Willie Chaney

Youth and the
Christ Way

BY

PROF. J. A. HUFFMAN, D. D.

Author of

*Young People and the Christ Life, With Christ in the
Deeper Lessons, A Guide to the Study of the Old
and New Testaments, Voices from Rocks and
Dust Heaps of Bible Lands, Biblical Con-
firmations from Archæology, etc.*

Published by

Standard Press, Marion, Indiana

DEDICATORY

❧ ❧ ❧ ❧ ❧

To all that great host of youth who passionately desire to find life's greatest happiness and largest measure of success, this volume is sincerely dedicated.

❧ ❧ ❧ ❧ ❧

* * * * * * * * *

THESIS

The Christ way, though rugged, makes a special appeal to the heroism of youth; holds the solution to all of youth's problems, and is the way of peace, happiness and success. This way may be found in youth, and followed from youth.

* * * * * * * * *

Contents

THE CHRIST WAY CONCERNING YOUTH'S HERITAGE

CHAPTER ONE

THE CHRIST WAY CONCERNING YOUTH'S HERITAGE

Every child has a right to be well-born; to have a heritage of physically, materially and spiritually good things. But this heritage is not realized by the majority of the young. In many parts of the world almost all these are denied them. The American youth has, however, on the average, a liberal endowment of the coveted good things. Since it is to the young people of America that this challenge is made, it is the Christ way in relation to our wonderful heritage that concerns us.

It is true that one must go elsewhere to see America as it really is. The good things are too many and too near us to be properly evaluated. It is only as we stand at a greater distance, and view them from an entirely different condition of affairs, that we discover our exceptional advantages.

Students of history have noted the great moral and spiritual chasm which separates the people of the United States and those of the countries southward, including Mexico, Central and South America. Tracing backward to locate the cause, it is discovered that the lands to the south were peopled by men in search of gold, while our beloved country was settled largely by those whose quest was God. The addition of one letter in the word "God" has made a world of difference in the history of a country and in the heritage of its generations.

It is not claimed that everything in America is as it should be. There are many things that are unideal, and even vicious. The prevalence of theft, murder, divorce, intemperance, Sabbath-breaking and other lawlessness is a sad commentary upon a great and free people. There is no alibi for this condition, except that we are living in an after-war-torn period, when four million men, who were taught constantly to kill, and only to kill, have been turned back upon society to release their depraved passions. The moral fibre of the nation has become seriously affected. The foreign elements which have been permitted to come to our shores, whose ideals have been entirely different from the American, have taken advantage of the morally and socially unsettled condition, and have sought to trample under feet our sacred institutions, and even to break down our government. But this is not true Americanism, it is the prostitution of a great and noble heritage.

The picture here described is dark and foreboding, especially to such as have lost faith entirely in humanity; certainly to those who have lost faith in God. Then, too, much has been said and written in complete disparagement of the rising generation. Though there is considerable ground for such pessimism, there are many reasons for optimism. The writer has not lost his faith in youth. His contact with many young people throughout the land has convinced him that there are, in the rising generation, many young people as noble, pure, earnest and good as any generation ever produced.

The way is open in America for the poor boy or girl to reach the top. There is nothing to hinder him. The only living ex-president of the United States was an orphaned country lad, Herbert Hoover, who was reared upon the plains of Iowa. An orphan of part Indian blood, Mr. Curtis, was Vice-President during the same administration. Not only in politics, but in industry and in the professions many have gone to the top, despite great handicaps. In the church of Christ, some of her most efficient and beloved leaders have arisen from among the humbler class. Such is the opportunity which America affords.

One does not need to travel far to discover that America is the envy of the world. He is surprised at the information which the people of other parts of the world have concerning America. Their conception of conditions here are not always correct, but they know much about America and her opportunities.

While travelling on a railroad train between Rome and Naples, a young Italian, who could speak a broken English, and who happened to be travelling in the same compartment, recognizing me as an American, engaged me in conversation. It became apparent that his purpose was to seek help in getting to America. If I could employ him, he might be placed upon the preferential list, and thus get ahead of others in the small Italian quota of annual immigrants which America permits. When I told him that I was not an employer of men, but an educator, somewhat playfully but in all seriousness, he said: "Mr., if you will take me with you to America, I will be your chauffeur as long as you live. Put me in your pocket or your grip—any way, just so you get me there." He was a handsome fellow, about thirty years of age, six feet tall, and informed me that he was an aviator in the employment of the Italian government, but only part time, because of the large number of aviators given employment. He said that he should like to have a wife and home, but could not earn enough money to make a living for himself. Upon further inquiry, he told me that there was no use for him to make application to come to America, unless he could get on the preferential list, as there were enough applicants to fill the Italian quota for American immigration for twenty years. Inquiry since has led me to believe that he was correct. The attitude of this young man illustrates the envy in which America is held by a very large part of the world.

In occasional periods of economic depression the people of America feel much wounded and abused. But few among us know anything like a real handicap. Most of the American people do not eat because they are hungry, but so that they do not become hungry, while there are millions of our own generation living elsewhere in the world, who have never had a square meal. They live and will die hungry. Our experience of need in our most serious and occasional periods of depression is theirs in multiplied form, constantly.

It would give us a greater appreciation of our heritage to know how people live in other parts of the world.

My guide said to me in Cairo, Egypt: "Maybe you wonder why there are so many people upon the streets," and proceeded to give the reason. "You see," said he, "the people of Egypt do not have homes, like you people have in America. If they did they would not be out here upon the streets in such great numbers." Upon making inquiry why there were so many people, apparently whole families, sitting along the streets in old Cairo, I was told that they had no other place to be. They had with them their small possessions, all that they had in the world.

Someone has said that, in visiting the Near East, the first and the last thing which one sees is the outstretched hand, and the first and last word one hears is "backsheesh", which means money. It is the language of the beggar, asking for help.

It is a common thing to meet on the dark and narrow streets of the Oriental city a tiny little tot, or groups of them, just old enough to walk about, holding out their dirty little hands, asking for help. They have been born in poverty, and are trained to be beggars.

Illustrating this condition of childhood were two little waifs whom I met upon the streets of Jerusalem one day. From a group of small children, there stepped out a little lad who appeared to be about four years of age. He was scantily clad: his face was dirty, and his hair was unkempt. Extending his poor, bony hand, he began to make a plea for help in fluent and almost eloquent manner. I could not understand a word that he was saying, but knew by his outstretched, open hand, what he was asking. Being interested to know what the little fellow was saying I asked an Arab, who was leading his bicycle along, to give attention and then to interpret it to me. Having listened to the boy as he repeated his plea, the Arab told me in his broken English what he had said. "He is telling you," said he, "that he has no father, no mother, nor anyone to take care of him, and that he is hungry. That he wants you to give him a half of a piaster (about two and a half cents). He says that, if you will give him a half of a piaster, God will give you long life. He will let you live to be ninety years old."

No sooner was the coin placed into the little fellow's hand than he bowed appreciatively and stepped aside. Immediately a little girl, about his age, apparently just as needy, stepped forward and made the same plea, also to receive a small coin. These little folks know nothing but need, and possibly never will know anything different.

The womanhood of America has many reasons for gratitude. There are few places in the world where women have the opportunity which is afforded them in America. In many European countries they are expected to work along with the men, doing the heavy work of the field and other labor, and in many other places the more menial tasks are assigned to them regularly by the customs of the country.

Observing the use to which the little donkey is put in the Near East, being compelled to carry all kinds of loads, sometimes big, heavy men, whose feet almost drag the ground as they ride them, the writer protested to a missionary in Syria, one day, that the donkey did not have a "square deal" in the Near East. To this the missionary readily assented. But one day while driving along the road we saw coming a very large load of unthreshed wheat. We knew that it was on the back of a camel, a donkey, or a person. When we came near enough we discovered that it was a woman who was carrying the burden. Seeing her, the missionary said: "You say that the donkey does not have a 'square deal' in the Near East. I say that the donkey comes nearer having a 'square deal' than the woman does." And my missionary friend was correct.

In Syria I saw highways in process of construction. Men would sit by the roadside, and with a heavy hammer, break the stone into the size needed for road building. When the broken stones were needed for construction purposes, women would carry them in baskets upon their heads or shoulders, and deposit them before the heavy roller which was used to crush them still more.

While the American youth has a great heritage economically and socially, there are those things which are of still greater value, the educational and religious.

For the greater part of the world's youth there are no provisions for education. The free, public school system is a luxury which the average American youth accepts as a matter of fact, but which is unknown by far the larger part of his generation. Though there may be lurking in a democratic form of government, such as ours, perils of which all should beware, every man is a king and every woman is a queen. Boys and girls are princes and princesses, and should evaluate their heritage accordingly.

Spiritually the American heritage is still greater. Our young people are descendants of parents whose quest has been for God, who were willing to face the perils of sea and dangers of a new country for the sake of religious freedom. In a land where church and state are forever separate, and where they were permitted to worship God in their own way, under their own vine and fig tree, they have reared their sons and daughters. The Bible is, or may be, in the hand of every American youth, in his mother tongue. There is scarcely a spiritual need of which anyone could dream which has not been provided in advance for every boy and girl.

The American youth has a great election, and the sooner he discovers it the better. To adequately evaluate this, and to properly relate himself to it is the ideal toward which he should earnestly strive.

The most practical and safest question to ask is: "What is the Christ way in relation to this great heritage?" "What would He have me be? What would He have me to do? What does He expect of me? How may I measure up to His standards for my life and conduct?" These are the real and worthy questions which should be answered by every young man and woman, every boy and girl.

This election is not one to privilege, but to responsibility. The word "opportunity" also spells accountability. To whom much is given, of him much is expected. God's measuring stick for men is always consistent with their light and ability.

THE CHRIST WAY IN YOUTH'S RELIGION

Chapter II

THE CHRIST WAY IN YOUTH'S RELIGION

The religion of the Bible is not a religion of adult-hood, as some would have us believe. The Bible is a universal book, and speaks in the terms of experience common to all men, of all ages, everywhere, but the appeal which it makes to youth is very impressive. If there is one class for whom the Bible has a special message, and to whom the religious appeal is especially directed, it is youth.

The founder of Christianity, Christ Himself, was busy about His Father's business at the age of twelve. He had a definite program which He fully knew, and from which He could not be deflected by even His dearest friend.

The relation of youth to Christianity is written all over the letters of Paul to Timothy, but there is one particular charge given to youth by this ablest exponent of Christianity which cannot escape our attention. Here it is: "Let no man despise thy youth; but be thou an ensample to them that believe, in word, in manner of life, in love, in faith, in purity."—1 Timothy 4:12.

This charge to youth appears almost overwhelming. Not only is youth expected to be all this for his own sake, but to be an ensample to believers of all ages in relation to these things. The first two things mentioned are intensely practical and cover the whole range of outward conduct, while the last three are fundamentally experiential, and are absolutely essential to the former. Being experientially right, so that we may be able to be practically right, is God's order for youth, as well as for others. If there were a single handicap to the religion of youth, either in its experiential or practical applications, this charge would be preposterous, and even tyrannical.

The closing word of this charge to youth is significant. It is the word "purity," not maturity. It would be too much to expect of youth maturity, which is an attainment and comes only with the ripening of the years; but purity, which is an obtainment, may be reasonably expected of youth. The apostle who gave this charge to his son in the Gospel must have had great confidence in the vigor of youthful religion, and in its ability to take its place even in the leadership of example.

John, the most aged of the apostles, assumed a similar attitude to youth when he gave one of the most remarkable challenges ever faced by the young. "I write unto you, young men, because ye have overcome the evil one." "I have written unto you, young men, because ye are strong, and the word of God abideth in you, and ye have overcome the evil one."—1 John 2: 13, 14.

The "strength of youth" has long been a familiar phrase, and appears as a befitting characterization. This is particularly true in the light of certain facts which force themselves upon us.

To the blushing shame of humanity, it must be said that the wars of all lands and of all times have been fought largely by the comparatively young. The procedure in the World War illustrates this fact. Even in the United States, after the available men in their early twenties had been enlisted, the call was issued, in descending scale, to those of younger age. In other lands the draft reached still more youthful levels than in our own country. It is a sad commentary upon our civilization, that the human race has sacrificed ten million young men of one generation upon the altar of war.

The reason for this demand for young men for war is evident. Young men are strong and courageous, and make better soldiers in every way.

In harmony with the recognized strength of youth, it is a fact that the maximum of physical strength and endurance is reached and passed quite early. In the case of the pugilist and athlete, it is probably somewhere between tweny-five and thirty years.

The strength of youth is also proven in other ways, as a review of the world's work shows. When the roll call is made of those who have achieved, many youthful faces appear. Only a few typical cases are necessary to illustrate this.

David beheaded the Philistine giant when he was but a "stripling."

Saul of Tarsus acted as the official referee of Stephen, the first Christian martyr, while yet in his twenties.

Timothy became the assistant to the great apostle Paul in his late teens.

Miriam served as custodian of the babe who was destined to be the world's greatest lawgiver when she was a youthful maiden.

Sir Isaac Newton discovered the law of gravitation at the age of twenty-one.

William Pitt was prime minister of England at the age of twenty-five.

David Livingstone was called to be the "Apostle to Africa" at twenty-one.

John Calvin completed his Theological Institutes at twenty-six.

William Cullen Bryant wrote his immortal "Thanatopsis" before he was eighteen.

George Fox became the leader of the Quakers at twenty-eight.

Helen Keller, with the handicap of being blind and deaf, and thus shut away from the world, graduated from college at the age of twenty-two, and had written three books by the time she was twenty-eight.

Marconi invented the wireless at twenty-six.

Charles Lindbergh flew the Atlantic Ocean before he had reached his twenty-sixth birthday.

It may be added that there is a serious doubt whether any considerable number of people have ever achieved anything out of the ordinary who did not definitely begin achieving when young. It is true that many do not succeed to the point of attracting particular attention until much later, but in those cases the die has been cast much earlier.

The Apostle, John, was not mistaken when he wrote to youth, "Ye are strong." The heroic in youth has been successfully appealed to in regard to other things, why not in relation to its higher and spiritual interests?

When the young discover the real challenge in religion, to the heroic, it will have a tremendous appeal for them. John knew human nature, and acted accordingly. There is enough in the religion of Jesus Christ to challenge the brainiest of the brainy and the brawniest of the brawny. I, too, write unto you young men because ye are strong.

The very fact of the strength of youth may become, in itself, a snare, if not properly reckoned with. The overestimating of one's own spiritual strength is a snare which needs to be guarded against by the Christian.

One does not need to know anything about the subject of religious psychology to discover that children are spiritually susceptible at a very early age. Observation and personal experience teach this. An occasional girl has been intelligently converted at the age of five years, and boys at approximately seven. Girls are slightly ahead of boys in physical, intellectual and spiritual development. These are not the average ages at which children attain to personal responsibility, but they do illustrate the very early age at which some children reach this period and become susceptible to conversion. Until this period is reached children do not need conversion, but are in the kingdom. Jesus said, as He took little ones into His arms and blessed them: "Suffer the little children, and forbid them not, to come unto me: for to such belongeth the kingdom of heaven."—Matt. 19: 13. He also used little children to typify the characteristics of those who are in the kingdom, for He said, "Except ye turn, and become as little children,

ye shall in no wise enter into the kingdom of heaven."
—Matt. 18:3.

A study of the psychology of religion has disclosed
the fact that the high points in the religious susceptibility of youth, on the average, are attained very
much earlier than is generally supposed; and that
when these high points are passed the likelihood of
conversion grows rapidly less. This is such a serious
matter that it deserves careful attention on the part
of youth for its own sake. It also demands attention
of every serious-minded youth and adult, for the sake
of others.

It has been a well-known and oft-quoted statistic,
that more than one-half of the people who ever become Christians are converted before they reach the
age of twenty, but it has been discovered that by far
the larger majority who ever become Christians are
converted in the early teen age.

The ages ten to twelve mark a distinctly high point
in the likelihood for conversion. Incidentally this cor-
responds to the age when Jesus was taken to the
temple, at twelve, at which time the Jewish lad was
made a "son of the law," and was held personally
responsible. It also marks the beginning of the ado-
lescent period in youth, when a physical change takes
place, and at which time there also occurs an intellectual quickening. The spiritual nature becomes
keenly susceptible, and conversion in this period is
quite likely. An investigation has disclosed the fact
that a fair percentage of the dependable laity and
of the outstanding, capable and trusted leaders in
the Church of Christ were converted at this period.

But there is another period in the lives of youth, when boys and girls meet each other on the highest pinnacle of religious susceptibility which they will ever attain. This age was given by older writers in the field of religious psychology as sixteen. This is scarcely a safe age to name now, in this time of increased light and better educational facilities. It would be a conservative estimate should the age of fifteen years be fixed as the highest pinnacle of youth's likelihood for conversion. Those of the present laity and leadership of the Church who were not converted at about the age of twelve, the first period of marked religious awakening, are almost certain to have been converted at about this age.

A very serious thing comes into consideration here. When this high point of religious susceptibility is passed and disregarded, a period of increasing indifference begins, and the likelihood of conversion rapidly decreases. So marked is this decline that, when the age of twenty-three is reached, the likelihood is no greater for conversion than at the age of seven, and the probability for conversion will never increase, but always decrease.

This study of youth forces certain conclusions which the wise will heed. To the unsaved boy or girl it should be a clarion call to yield to Christ for salvation. To the parent, Sunday School teacher and minister it should serve as a challenge to the most heroic and sacrificing effort to bring young people into the fold of Christ before they reach the toboggan slide of unlikelihood for conversion, and go down upon the other side.

Reckoning with the gradual decrease in religious susceptibility after the teen age has been left, it is observed that between twenty and thirty years a small percentage of people are converted; between thirty and forty a smaller percentage; between forty and fifty a still smaller percentage; and that when the line of fifty years is crossed, only now and then one person who has never been converted becomes a Christian. A careful investigation discloses that of those who reach the age of twenty-three years, having never made any profession of religion, only two out of one hundred will ever do so, leaving ninety-eight who never will. One of America's most favorably known, and best informed, evangelists is authority for the statement that out of fifteen thousand persons who have attained the age of sixty-five years, who have never made any profession of religion, nor have been identified with the people of God in any way, only one will ever do so, leaving fourteen thousand nine hundred and ninety-nine who never will.

The real situation, as it pertains to young people and religion, can best be seen by use of an illustration.

We had heard that somewhere in the Niagara River, above the Falls, there is a place or point called, "Redemption Point," up to which boats with their occupants, caught in the swift upper rapids, had been rescued, but past which none had ever drifted and been saved from the Falls. No one visiting Niagara can fail to be impressed with the racing, tumbling, foaming waters of the upper rapids, and the great cataract just below.

A few summers since, the writer stood upon the

edge of the Falls, watching the water make its tremendous plunge, and listening to its thunderous roar. Occasionally a breeze wafted a spray of mist into his face. While standing there he remembered what he had heard concerning "Redemption Point" in the upper rapids.

Being somewhat curious, he decided to go in quest for the interesting place, by following along the bank upon the American side. Having gone the distance of something like a quarter of a mile, he met a group of workmen, with whom he stopped and made inquiry. After hanging their heads for a few moments, one of them became the spokesman of the group and said: "Yes, I know where 'Redemption Point' is, but, Mister, that is miles up the river." "Miles up the river?" The inquirer had expected to find it down very near the Falls.

It was a hot day in June. The writer was alone, and could not have found the place, neither would he have been able to identify it, had he walked those miles up the stream. He went back and sat down under a tree, by the edge of the rapids, near the Falls, and meditated. It was an epoch-marking experience and hour. He had studied religious psychology: he knew the statistics presented above, but he had never vitalized them. " 'Redemption Point' far up the stream!" Yes, it was so not only in the Niagara, but in the real stream of life. Destinies are fixed early—so much earlier than is ordinarily believed. If we would rescue souls, we should do it before Redemption Point is passed. Something happened that day which gave to the writer a changed emphasis upon his religious efforts. He was determined that, in the future, the major part of his time and energy should be expended upon young life, that period of life where redemption is more likely. The impression and challenge of that day had a bearing upon his decision to devote himself to the work of Christian education, and even upon the writing of this volume.

In emphasizing the advantage and desirability of devoting time and energy to the young, it is not intended that less effort shall be expended upon people of later life, rescue missions and such like. Rather, a challenge is thrown out to all who have to do with young life, to bring them into the fold of Christ while they are impressionable and may be won; also to have them saved, not only for an eternity of bliss, but for a life of service.

It was Marion Lawrence who said that the saving of an old person is the saving of a unit, a soul, which is worth more than a world; but the saving of a boy or a girl is the saving of a multiplication table, which will go on multiplying down through the years. We should not seek souls only, but souls, plus lives.

Lest our illustration of the Redemption Point in the Niagara rapids should appear too pessimistic, the following incident may be reckoned with.

Since the experience described above, the writer stood one day upon the eastern shore of the island which lies in the Niagara, just above the Falls, called "Goat Island." Looking up stream he saw something which appeared like a part of a scow. Upon inquiry he was told the following story:

Some time previous, some workmen up stream were

caught in the current, and despite their attempts to land, drifted down past "Redemption Point" and still on down towards the Falls. They were being tossed hopelessly by the dashing waters. The nearer they approached the cataract, the smaller their hope for rescue became. They were clinging fearfully to their small craft, with no apparent chance for their lives. All at once the scow was tossed between two jagged rocks, where it became tightly wedged.

From the shore these men were heard by their cries. They knew not how soon another swelling wave might lift them from their moorings, and send them down over the precipice.

Frantic efforts were made for their rescue, seamen, firemen and civilians cooperating on both sides of the rapids. By heroic and danger-defying work, while women screamed and fainted, the men were eventually brought safely to land. A few persons had, at great risk and expense, been saved from the cataract, after having passed "Redemption Point."

Those very few persons rescued symbolize the scarcity of those who are saved near the close of life; also the difficulty and cost of saving them. The lesson of this incident should seriously impress everyone who learns of it.

The importance of the religion of youth was recognized even in pre-Christian days. That children should honor their parents was the fifth commandment of the Decalogue (Ex. 20:12), and was the first of the commandments to the keeping of which was attached a promise—that of long life.

The writer of Ecclesiastes wrote thus to youth: "Remember also thy Creator in the days of thy youth, before the evil days come, and the years draw nigh, when thou shalt say, I have no pleasure in them."— Eccl. 12:1. Then follows a most pathetically pictur- esque description of decrepit old age, and the conclu- sion of the whole matter is declared: "Fear God, and keep His commandments; for this is the whole duty of man."—Eccl. 12:13.

The writers of the Book of Proverbs addressed most of their maxims of wisdom and counsel to the young. Five of the first seven chapters of The Proverbs are addressed directly to "My son," and one of the seven to "My sons." The last chapter of the book is also addressed to "My sons." The intervening chapters are all indirectly directed to youth. What a remarkable emphasis upon the importance of the religion of youth!

In the light of the foregoing considerations, it can be easily seen that for the vast majority of people the choice is made between the "religion of youth," or no religion at all. Days, weeks, months and years put such great distances between people and their Savior that they will not retrace, even though a loving God would save them if they would but re- turn. It is not fair to man's Creator to expend youth- ful and adult strength in leading a life of selfishness and sin, and then, when standing upon the verge of the grave, to fling into His face the dregs of a misspent life. Those who seek the Lord early shall find Him. Those who do not seek Him early are likely never to do so.

The theory that young people must become outbroken

sinners to become good saints is an abominable belief. "Bigger sinner: better saint," has never been true. The risk of letting young people get far away, so that the change brought about in their lives when rescued by high pressure evangelistic methods may be more radical and marked, is too dangerous to concede. The fact is that every child who comes to the age of personal responsibility is a big enough sinner, and has tasted enough of sin, to become the best saint Heaven demands.

That young people are capable of definite and exemplary religious experiences is proven by the Scriptures, as well as by their own testimony. Experiences differ, not only between youth and adulthood, but between adults themselves. While there is general agreement in the matter of religious experience between all classes, it is only fair to say that there are no two experiences quite alike.

The demonstrations of religious experiences differ according to temperament and training. Too much importance should not be attached to any particular mode of demonstration. A silent tear coursing the cheek of one may be as religiously significant in one case as a boisterous burst of ecstasy in the case of another. It is genuineness which counts, and God judges that from the heart.

One thing which is not likely to be overstressed is that young people must have a religious experience of their own. To have been reared in a nominally Christian land, and in a Christian home, is not sufficient, much as these are to be prized. The only safeguard against the rising tide of infidelity and atheism is a personal knowledge of the saving grace of Jesus Christ. Nothing less than this is the Christ way in relation to the religious experiences of the young.

Then, too, a definite experience in grace is necessary to make the Christ way in the practices of life possible. It is not enough to idealize or even to ask the question what the Christ way would be in relation to the affairs of life. There must be supplied a dynamic to enable young people, as well as others, to live the Christ way. It is not only "What would Jesus have me do?" but also, "What will He help me do?" Saving help and keeping power must come from a source apart from ourselves, and it is the very genius of the Christian religion to supply these. A program of *doing,* without the prerequisite of *being,* is certain to break down.

The crises of the religious life are not only more likely to be met by the young, but are more easily met. It is easier to surrender before the rebellion of sin has become a fixed attitude. Consecration is less difficult to him who has not hardened himself in his own way. Early consecration is youth going into Canaan at Kadesh-barnea. And Kadesh-barnea, the first place Canaan is reached, is still the place where God would have His people enter. Israel turned aside, and wasted many precious years in wilderness wandering, and then those who entered at all had to come in by way of the swelling Jordan.

Neither is there here suggested any easy religious way for youth to travel. This would be unbecoming to those who are challenged as "strong." Repentance for sin must be genuine and thorough, if forgiveness is expected. Consecration must be complete and final, if the sanctified life would be entered. Because these crises are more likely and more easily met in youth does not argue that they are less real. The lad who wades the Mississippi River where it is narrow, near its source, is just as truly on the other side as the man who ferries across, at its mouth, where it is several miles wide. The Israelites would have been in Canaan as truly had they entered at Kadesh, as they were when they entered later by a more difficult route. They would have had the same blessings of Canaan, plus the advantages which an earlier entrance would have given them. The crises should be, and will be sufficiently marked, if they are really met by youth. But it is not so much the crisis itself, as the life which is marked by the crisis, in which we need to be interested. What a wonderful thing it is to save a soul! But more wonderful is it to save that soul, plus the life with all its ransomed powers. This is the opportunity which is offered to youth.

Youth has its peculiar way of expressing its religious life. It will speak, but is more likely to act. Give it a chance, and it is surprising what the religion of youth will accomplish. It may philosophize less, but may achieve more. One of the wisest things that any pastor and church can do is to give youth an outlet for its religious life.

Too long has youth been told that it is the church of tomorrow: it has grown tired of this. What Christian youth wants to feel is that it is not only the church of tomorrow, but at least a part of the church of today. The Christ way in relation to youth's place in

His church is not to make them leaders, but to gives them something to do, and this youth eagerly desires. If churches and pastors could only discover it, there is enough work to be done for Christ to fully occupy every adult and young person within its group.

The religion of youth is essentially the same as that of adulthood, differing only in its advantages, its manifestations and expressions. Let us pray that God may give, both to youth and adulthood, the vision of the glorious possibilities of the Christ way in youth's religion.

THE CHRIST WAY IN YOUTH'S EDUCATION

Chapter III

THE CHRIST WAY IN YOUTH'S EDUCATION

Much as has been said and written upon the subject of education, it still remains challenging. Because of the successive generations which follow each other, and the ever-changing conditions, the subject is perennial.

Youth and education must always be related, for youth is the time when education, in the commonly accepted meaning of the term, can be pursued. It is the time when knowledge can be more easily acquired and retained. It is the period preceding that of adulthood, when the training which may be had in youth is greatly needed. Reckoning with the importance of living, and the preparation necessary to the right kind of living, there must be a Christ way in relation to youth's education.

Just as certain as it pays to prepare the ground before sowing the seed, to discipline the twig as it should grow, to polish the precious stone before putting it on the market, or to sharpen the tools before using them, just so does the education of the young pay. There has never been a time in the history of the world when such demands have been made upon oncoming youth as now. The very best preparation which youth may obtain is none too good. The leaders of any generation must meet that generation upon its own plane, and must give evidence of being equal in every way, and superior in some ways, for human nature resents the leadership of equality, and absolutely revolts at proposed leadership of inferiority.

It is not here assumed that every young man and woman should go to college. It is insisted, however, that those who expect to make any particular impress upon their fellows must be trained and capable. Since these lines are especially addressed to Christian young people, and since the world is so sadly in need of genuine Christian leadership in every legitimate field of endeavor, a challenge is here intended for Christian young people to provide that leadership for their generation.

The school is the child of religion. Our public school system can be traced back to the Jewish synagogue, where the child was instructed in the primary subjects of education, with special reference to religion. In the early history of America, the school grew up around the church, with the Bible as the chief textbook in the New England schools. The early American colleges were organized, maintained and operated by the church. They were conducted largely for the sake of preparing young people for the sacred callings, and their original charters show Christianity had a very prominent place in early American education, and the greatness of the American nation resulted.

Gradually, however, the state has assumed the responsibility of educating its citizenship, and the objective has shifted, much to the neglect of the original aim. The Christ way in youth's education becomes a very serious consideration, if youth are to be saved, and future generations made secure through them.

Training the intellect is a religious matter, for religion is not a matter of the heart only, as some would insist. It is a matter of the heart, but more, for Jesus answering the question of the Pharisees, concerning the greatest commandment said: "Thou shalt love the Lord thy God with all thy heart, and with all thy soul, and with all thy *mind,* and with all thy strength."—Mark 12:30. Upon the authority of Jesus, religion is a matter of both head and heart. Head and heart are not necessarily pitted against each other. God gave us both our heads and our hearts, and they are very near each other. He intended that we should use both of them.

In an address before other school men, a prominent educator recently declared that to train the intellect in the secrets of certain scientific subjects of the educational curriculum, without developing a proper moral attitude to the use of these powers, is a dangerous thing. And the speaker was right. To neglect the moral and religious element in education is a serious blunder. To educate a dangerous man more highly is to make him more dangerous. While not so serious in results, it is also pathetic when right heart attitudes are developed, and the mind is not trained to function harmoniously and adequately. To be theoretically and doctrinally right in relation to the great fundamentals of the Christian faith is exceedingly important. Heart and head should be trained together, and both of them should be employed in loving and serving God. This is the Christ way in the education of youth.

Education is a thing not easily defined, and in vain we may seek for a perfectly satisfactory definition. One outstanding educator has defined education as, "The knowledge of one's environment, and the ability to adapt one's self to that environment." Another equally prominent educator has criticized this definition, declaring that education implies all that is mentioned, but more, that it includes the ability to adapt environment to one's self. In other words, education does not make persons creatures of environment only, but also creators of environment. This criticism is just, and corrects and enriches the first attempted definition.

A working definition, then, of education embraces three things:

A knowledge of one's environment.

The ability to adapt one's self to his environment.

The ability to adapt environment to one's self.

Man's environment is composed of three things, and under these three heads may be catalogued everything which makes up human experience. Beginning at the most tangible, man's first environment is that of material *things*.

The floor upon which we stand, the chair upon which we sit, the desk upon which we lay our hands, the walls about us, the roof over our heads—beginning just here and reaching out into the unmeasured space of the universe, is man's material environment.

To know this environment precipitates at once into the study of the physical and biological sciences:

physics, chemistry, geology, astronomy, biology, zoology and botany. If education requires a knowledge of man's material environment, and some service to it and from it, the challenge is confessedly great, for here are vast fields to explore.

Our next environment is that of *people*. To know this environment leads directly into the study of humanity and the human relationships: anthropology, history, sociology, economics and civics. All the human relationships are included in the curriculum of such a course. If man's material environment is great and challenging, this one exceeds just in the measure that people are of more importance than things.

Last, but by no means least, of man's environments, is *God*. To begin to know God is to open the vast field of spiritual knowledge. Theology, the doctrine of God; hamartiology, the doctrine concerning sin; soteriology, the doctrine of salvation—these high-sounding subjects come within the sphere of knowledge of man's greatest environment—God.

It can easily be seen that any process of education which leaves out God is lopsided and inadequate. The Christ way in education is to put first things first. Ruling God out of the educational process is gradually destroying the moral fibre of the young, and is paganizing the institutions of higher learning. Here is one of the strongest arguments for the maintenance of the Christian College, at any cost. The Christ way in education cannot be overlooked without serious consequences.

There are at present some encouraging signs appearing upon the educational horizon. Educators all over the country are beginning to discover the inadequacy and shortcomings of an educational system which omits the religious element, and are beginning to voice the need for a better program, in no unmistakable terms.

A short time ago, the director of Normal Training in one of the midwestern states rapped at the door of the writer's study, and engaged him in very interesting conversation. He said that he was becoming convinced that the present process of public education was failing to do for the rising generation what it should, because of which there is in evidence a moral breakdown. He declared his belief that religious instruction should be brought back into the public schools, and before he left he had secured from the writer a promise to outline a course in Biblical instruction for public school teachers. This course was prepared, and approved by the State Board of Education, and became a part of the elective curriculum of that state for teacher training.

Soon after the outlining of the above-mentioned course, the writer was engaged by the High School Teachers' Association of the same state to prepare a text for the study of the Bible in the High Schools of the state, as an elective for credit. This text was adopted by the State Board of Education, and the book, "A Guide to the Study of the Old and New Testaments," is being used in many states of the Union, in High Schools, Academies, Bible Schools, Junior Colleges, and Colleges.

From these facts we discover that the lost Bible is being restored, in some small measure at least, to the public schools. The Christ way in relation to the American youth is being inquired after.

Recently six hundred leading educators of the world met in New York City to observe the one hundredth anniversary of the founding of New York University. Alfred Noyes, celebrated English poet, told these educators that the first great need of modern education is to "recover faith in God." Addressing himself to advocates of the modern type of education, Mr. Noyes said: "Ye have taken away my Lord, and I know not where ye have laid him."

But it is not only from educators that the challenge is coming, for the restoration of the religious element in the instruction of young people. Business men, scientists, and statesmen are letting their pleas and preachments be heard.

In a recent article in the Wall Street Journal, the voice of finance, the following significant paragraph was found: "What this country needs is not a greater Navy or Standing Army; not so much more irrigation or forest reservation. It needs more the sort of religion our fathers and mothers used to have—the kind that considers it good business to stop work a bit earlier on Prayer Meeting night; that believes the house of God is the proper place for our young people on the Sabbath Day, and that Family Worship is a custom too important to be forgotten."

Recently Roger Babson, noted statistician and economist, said: "As Americans we have put too much faith in material things, on money making, and we have neglected our spiritual reserves. In the present crisis we have been hard hit by financial losses and unemployment. But, worst of all, we have been caught spiritually bankrupt."

The same Mr. Babson asked the great electrical engineer, Charles Steinmetz, shortly before his death, what would be the greatest developments in the next fifty years. To this question Mr. Steinmetz replied: "The great discoveries of the next generation will be along spiritual lines. Here is the field where miracles are going to occur. We scientific men have spent our lives studying physical forces. We have made the most sensational discoveries in the history of the world. And our knowledge has not brought happiness. People are fed up on material things. What America needs now is a development of the spiritual side of life."

Thomas A. Edison was visited by Mr. Babson, during the early part of the last year of Mr. Edison's life. When asked what new and radical inventions he expected within the next few years, Mr. Edison turned to his visitor and said: "Mr. Babson, I do not pose as a preacher; but let me tell you that if there is a God, He will not let us advance much further materially until we catch up spiritually. A great fundamental law of science is that all forces must be kept in balance." This is only another and scientific way of expressing the Christ way in education.

A former member of a President's Cabinet recently said: "The soup line is not enough. A man's spirit must be saved, as well as his body. The American ideal should be far higher than that men should be well fed and selfish and satisfied, like cows on long grass."

Permit two of our latest Presidents to be heard upon this subject. The late Calvin Coolidge, after retiring to private life, in a copyrighted article published in the newspapers, wrote: "Outside the teachings of religion there is no answer to the problems of life. Our international and social relations cannot be solved by material forces. . . . . What is needed is a change of mind, a change of attitude toward the use of these material things, and toward each other. The real problems of the world are not material, but spiritual."

Herbert Hoover, in an address to a Baltimore convention of the National Federation of Men's Bible Classes, read by his secretary, wrote: "There is no other book so various as the Bible, nor one so full of consecrated wisdom. . . . As a nation we are indebted to the Book of books for our national ideals and representative institutions. Their preservation rests in adhering to its principles."

It is to God that we are to study to show ourselves approved workmen, no matter into what field of endeavor we enter. It is the truth that makes free. The Christ way in the education of youth is to pursue a curriculum well balanced in relation to all of man's environment, but with particular reference to his greatest environment, God. Educators, business men, scientists and statesmen are beginning to lament the absence of the moral and spiritual in the educational process, and are demanding that it be restored.

Throughout the world, but particularly in America, is there a rising tide in evidence in the matter of education. New standards of intelligence are being insisted upon. Our compulsory system of education, with mimimum school ages, varying from twelve to sixteen or even eighteen years, presents a great opportunity for young life—not only so, but it constitutes a great challenge to those who have young life with which to deal, to furnish wise and adequate leadership. Here is a tremendous possibility for Christian young people, and one which carries with it a responsibility of equal proportion. The hope of the world lies in the youth who will arise to the situation, who will obtain thorough preparation, who will place all upon the altar of consecration, and who will go out to exemplify the world's only salvation. Here is the Christ way in a complex, difficult and exacting age.

From our working definition of education with its inclusive fields, it must be evident to all thoughtful persons, that what we call education must, of necessity, be relative. No one can hope to possess more than a small fraction of the sum total of knowledge. Thomas Edison may have been a bit too pessimistic when, upon his eighty-second birthday he said: "We do not know one-millionth of one per cent of anything," but it does remain true that what any one person knows is so little compared to what there is to know, that it bulks insignificantly small.

This fact once discovered functions in keeping both young and old humble. There is no such thing as a "finished" education. There are tiny milestones which mark the way, but no one is really finished, educationally. There is one possible exception to this, it is the person who thinks that he is "finished." When one comes to such a conclusion, he is "finished," no matter whether he has graduated from the common school, or not.

In fact, one of the evidences of progress in real education is for one to have made the discovery of how very little he knows. The rank and file of people have not gone far enough to discover how much there is to know, therefore, how little, comparatively, they do know.

Here is an illustration from personal experience. In an institution of higher education, which the writer attended, there was a member of the faculty who was especially brilliant. He was one of those "star" professors who shone out with exceptional lustre among others of lesser magnitude. That institution is to be pitied which does not have one such.

That his words may be the more appreciated, it should be said that he was a man of about seventy winters, whose hairs were almost as white as snow. He had come by the educational route from the primer class to the Ph. D. degree, and had taught in that institution for thirty years. Sometimes he would become very eloquent in his lectures before his classes, resulting in wonderful times of inspiration.

One day, this Professor was discussing the vast fields of knowledge which remain unconquered. Step, by step, he led us, in our fancy, until we stood upon one of the highest peaks of the world. "See," said he, "these vast, unexplored fields of knowledge which stretch far out beyond the range of vision. There is much beyond that we cannot see. I want you boys to take a good look at these vast reaches, and then to go in and possess them." His words thus far were inspirational and challenging, but his next utterance was startling: "I want you to go in and occupy these fields, but, as for me, I shall be compelled to stop here at the bars." He "to stop at the bars?" If he, with all his learning and experience must stop at the bars, so we thought, we had not as yet seen "the bars." It was a lesson concerning the relativity of knowledge which cannot soon be forgotten.

Lest a wrong impression may be given, let it be added, that while all knowledge is relative, and we know only in part, that comparatively small amount of knowledge which we have, no matter within which realm of man's environment, that little may be well and assuredly known. It so occurs that the paradoxical happens. God has arranged it that knowledge concerning material things, which appears easier and more certain, recedes and takes second place, compared to the knowledge concerning spiritual things, when once we discover man's whole environment and the real meaning of education. This is the Christ way in the education of youth, if we but find it.

President E. Burritt Bryan once asked in a College Commencement Address the question: "When is a person truly educated?" He then proceeded to outline the answer as follows: It is

When one's body is trained;
When one's mind is functioning;
When one's spiritual life is aflame.

He then stopped suddenly, and dramatically said: "I did not mean to say that one is truly educated when his body is trained; when his mind is functioning; when his spiritual life is aflame. I only meant to say that, when all this obtains, a person is on the way to being educated."

But knowledge, though relative and limited, has a definite value. This value is economic and otherwise. Statistics on a subject of this kind can possibly be only relatively accurate, and must change from time to time, therefore, are not to be taken too dogmatically, but they should be permitted to teach us their lesson.

Dean Lord, of Boston University, is authority for the following statistics concerning the value of education.

The economic value of a common school education, distributed over the average lifetime, is forty-five thousand dollars.

The economic value of a high school education, above that of a common school education, is thirty-three thousand dollars, making a combined value of seventy-eight thousand dollars.

A college education enhances the economic value of a lifetime, including common school and high school, to the handsome figure of one hundred and fifty thousand dollars. These figures express in material terms the value of education. It is as though there were placed into the hand of a youth, upon his graduation from common school, the amount of forty-five thousand dollars; upon his high school graduation, another thirty-three thousand; and upon his college graduation, still another sum of seventy-two thousand dollars. There is one great difference, however, between education and money. According to the statistics of Life Insurance companies, the average inheritance in money is expended within seven years, some persons retaining it a longer, some a shorter period of time. Education is something which is infinitely superior to money, for it is one thing which thieves cannot steal, and which cannot be easily lost.

But education is not to be estimated in the terms of economic value only. It has a greater and higher value, that of service. Dean Lord is also authority for the following interesting estimate of education, in what he calls "distinguished service."

Of one million persons who have not completed the common school, six will have rendered distinguished service.

Of one million persons who have an elementary education, or have completed the common school, twenty-four will render distinguished service.

Of one million persons who have graduated from high school, six hundred twenty-three will render distinguished service.

Of one million persons who have graduated from college, five thousand seven hundred sixty-eight will render distinguished service.

Following the mathematics of the subject a little further, it will be seen that the elementary school graduate has his chances for distinguished service multiplied twenty-eight (plus) times by going on to high school graduation, and that college graduation multiplies the high school graduate's chances for distinguished service by nine (plus) times.

There is a book called "Who's Who in America." This book contains 29,704 sketches of the lives of those persons who are well known because of their achievements. The person who cannot read or write has one chance in 150,000 to get his name in this book; the grammar school graduate one in 4,250; the high school graduate one in 1,600; the college graduate one in 180; the honor student in college one in three.

Less than one per cent of American men are college graduates. Yet this one per cent has furnished fifty-five per cent of our Presidents, thirty-six per cent of our Members of Congress, forty-seven per cent of the Speakers of the House, fifty-four per cent of our Vice-Presidents, sixty-two per cent of Secretaries of State, fifty per cent of Secretaries of the Treasury, sixty-seven per cent of our Attorneys-General, and sixty-nine per cent of Justices of the Supreme Court.

The foregoing facts should constitute an irresistible challenge to young people who know them. Ministers, Sunday school teachers, parents, teachers and guardians should have them at their finger tips, so as to employ them in steadying youth in that period of upheavals, during the teen age, when they so sorely need it. Many a boy, and an occasional girl, has come home from school, likely high school, thrown down the armful of books and declared against another day of school.

Youth is constantly exposed to the temptation that the rewards of education do not justify the hard work required to secure it.

If they could but realize the value of education, particularly for service, drudgery would become a pleasure and hard tasks a delight that a thorough education might be obtained.

But it is the Christ way in relation to education—

the obtaining, and the use of it, in which we are concerned.

Thoroughly Christian young people are needed in all the legitimate occupations and professions of life. Certainly the sacred callings must have them. They must also be trained so as to be able to do the work in which they engage. "Study to show thyself approved unto God," is a command originally given to a young man in the Gospel ministry, but comes to all who have any part in the work of God, ministry and laity alike, in these challenging days.

That young people need a thorough training is self-evident. That this preparation should be secured in an institution where faith is not violated, but enlarged and enriched, is imperative. Here is the unanswerable argument for institutions of higher education where Christian young people may be prepared for their life work in an atmosphere which is safe and wholesome.

The state universities, and some others, are not only unchristian, but are actually becoming pagan. The faith of many a young person has been ruined in institutions of this kind. Those who know these institutions best know how just this severe indictment.

One of the most eloquent pleas which the author ever heard, on behalf of the Christian College, was made by the President of a great state university, who was himself a minister, but who confessed the helplessness of the state university to give to young people the thing which they need most—the cultivation of the religious life.

To the young people of America a veritable fortune

is offered in their educational opportunities. They may not only be enriched in their economic values, but enlarged also, and at the same time, in their capacities for service. Here is an election, not only to privilege, but to responsibility, for opportunity also means responsibility.

It is befitting that we should pause a moment to discover who the contributors are to such a fortune as this.

First, the home makes the largest contribution. Secondly, the state adds its part. Thirdly, the church pays the balance, particularly if education is Christian, as it should be.

Young people should know that the cost of their education in the average Christian College is from two to three times as much as they pay for their instruction. The Christian College matches every dollar paid by young people for tuition with from one to two dollars, which it must secure from those interested in educating young people in a Christian way, in order that youth may have this preparation for life. If this were not so, a college education would be absolutely prohibitive to all except the rich.

The challenge to education still exists and increases. The fields which education has discovered are still very much unoccupied. An excursion into one or the other of these fields discloses more territory lying beyond. No generation ever faced greater challenges than the one just rising. It may have seemed that most of the discoveries have been made; that most of the achievements have been accomplished; that most of the work is done, but such is not the case.

No matter which field is chosen, or is providentially assigned, in that field will be found enough to challenge the wisest of the wise and the strongest of the strong.

In the field of material things much remains yet to be accomplished. This field will not be conquested until every kind of known energy can be transformed into every other kind of energy. We are told by scientists that enough energy falls upon the earth's surface, in the form of light, every twenty-four hours, which, if it could be transformed into power, would run the mills and the factories of the world for twenty thousand years.

We are also told that a ton of coal contains a thousand times more energy than we get out of it by burning it, according to our present method.

Scientists have also discovered that all matter is composed of molecules, atoms and electrons. Of these we speak very glibly, as though we were familiar with them. But the fact is that only an occasional scientist has yet professed to have actually isolated a single atom from all the rest of atoms, so as to have actually discovered an atom.

Why do not those who are at liberty to enter into the field of material things enter and conquest? Why does not someone transform the energy of light into power to run our factories, and into heat to supply our homes? Why does not someone lead the way to the securing of those other nine hundred and ninety-nine parts of energy from that ton of coal? Why does not someone become really acquainted with the atom, and introduce him to the rest of us?

In the field of man's environment, that of people, a tremendously big task beckons. In an after-war-torn world, human relationships appear grossly estranged. The "war to end all wars" has been fought, but wars are still persistent. Thrones have crumbled and crowns have faded; a more satisfactory social relationship between the peoples of the world has been promised, but the sceptres have merely passed into other hands. If it is in this field where we may serve, the challenge is great, beginning in the tiniest community, and radiating to the ends of the earth.

From the field of spiritual things comes the greatest challenge of all. It is the challenge of securing a right relationship of man with God, through the Savior, Jesus Christ.

The population of the globe numbers more than one billion seven hundred millions, or more than seventeen hundred million souls. Of these, just about one billion persons, of our own generation, have never heard the name of Christ; have never had the opportunity of believing in Him. What a great challenge comes from this vast spiritual field! Shall we accept it?

Summarizing briefly, the Christ way in youth's education is that these great fields should be discovered. Youth should be provided with the very best preparation possible. That preparation should be secured in such an environment that his faith be not destroyed, but increased. One or the other of these great fields should be entered, as God Himself leads, and conquests should be carried on in the name of Jesus Christ, and to the glory of God.

THE CHRIST WAY IN YOUTH'S RECREATION

Chapter IV

THE CHRIST WAY IN YOUTH'S RECREATION

There is a Christ way in relation to everything which is right, whether it pertains to youth or adulthood. While play belongs especially to youth, it may have a larger place in the whole of life than is sometimes conceded. Occasionally some person is found who appears almost wholly devoid of appreciation of play even in relation to youth, but such persons are happily in the tiny minority and need not be considered. No apology is necessary in approaching a discussion of the Christ way in relation to the play life of youth.

To childhood play is perfectly natural. The child who does not play is not normal. It is beautiful to see little lambs playing upon the hillsides, jumping and skipping; but it is just as natural and even more beautiful to see little children at innocent play.

Play is necessary to the physical and intellectual well-being of the child. Of course, all unconsciously to him, his muscles are developed, bodily functions are exercised in a healthful manner, and the intellectual powers are gradually advanced while he plays.

Play is decidedly educational. In a way frequently overlooked, not only certain inherent instincts are cultivated, but a definite bearing upon future life is brought about. The motherly instinct of the little girl is developed while she plays with her doll, and the companion instinct is given opportunity for the asserting of itself as the little fellow romps with his dog. But beyond these natural instincts, play has often left its imprint upon later life, and later life has furnished a splendid commentary upon play, because of the close relation between the two. It is said that Florence Nightingale, "England's Angel of Pity," the young society girl, who when yet in her teens visited the cottages of the peasants and ministered to their sick, who later studied nursing in England, Germany and France, and subsequently took charge of the nursing of the wounded soldiers of the Crimean war numbering as many as ten thousand at a time, began her training for this great work as a little girl at play. She would play that her dolls were ill, and would nurse them; that some frightful accidents had befallen them, and would bandage their legs and arms with strips of linen, and treat them with greatest care. It is said that her first living patient was a dog whose wounds she dressed and bandaged.

It is unwise and well-nigh criminal to crush, in children, such a natural, necessary and God-given instinct as play. God intended that children should play, otherwise it would not be their natural, innocent and helpful heritage. Children should be taught to play as Christians, both as to kind and manner, what and how, but be permitted and encouraged to play for their own well-being and for the glory of Him who created them.

When we come to the play life of youth, there are certain other elements which must be reckoned with, but the same conditions largely maintain. Youth is childhood advanced, but it is not adulthood. It may be considered as the period of the upper grades, the high school and the college. What has been said concerning the physical and educational value of play in the childhood period is largely true in the period of youth. To youth it still remains natural to play. There has been for him no dividing line between childhood and youth, and he is still in some sense a child, a little older and a little bigger. The same disposition to play remains. Of course, growing responsibility has cut down his time to play, and his hours must be a little more jealously husbanded, but for him, "All work and no play" would still "make Jack a dull boy." To him the periods of play help to make tolerable the periods of work, both physically and otherwise.

There is added another value, a spiritual one, to play, in the period of youth. It is that of learning to do team work or to cooperate. This element was present, in some measure, in the play life of childhood, but becomes a prominent factor of decidedly spiritual value in the play of youth. It is the element which is present by virtue of necessity in the family group, where children are compelled to tolerate each other, to share and to cooperate with each other. This necessity is forced upon children sometimes as a blessing in disguise, because of poverty or near poverty which compels most rigid team work or cooperation. Some of the greatest men and women have been developed in the midst of such circumstances. In the play life of youth the matter of team work takes on a new element of voluntariness, which is another step in the direction of preparation for life's responsibilities in the midst of an increasingly complex society.

It is not difficult to detect the men and women who have never learned the lesson of team work. Some otherwise splendid people are crippled in their usefulness, because of their inability to cooperate. They are sometimes in evidence in student bodies, and are to be found not only in the occupations and professions, but even in the sacred callings. What a pity that good men and women should be hindered in their life work because they have never learned the lesson of cooperation! A wisely-directed play life in youth does not save from selfishness; it takes purity of heart to do that. But a proper play life will help to cultivate, even those whose heart motives are right, in the direction of a larger usefulness because of the spiritual value of cooperation.

The play life, like many other good things, needs regulation. This is particularly true because of the fact that the immature and less tutored are the principals in it. Even good things, not properly used and regulated, may become harmful. Especially is the regulation of the play life necessary, if harmony and proper relation is sought between piety and spirituality and the play life.

Play naturally begins within the home. It is here that the tiny tot makes its debut into the great world of activity, in the forms of play. Proper articles for play should be provided as the little folks develop, all the while discriminating against such toys and games as will cultivate wrong impressions and tendencies. As the toys gradually give place to games, care should be exerted that "pastimes" of a harmless kind are provided, and that play be conducted in a thoroughly honest and Christian manner. The general line to be drawn between harmful and harmless games is that which separates the games of chance from those of an educational type, or of skill. This is true, whether it be in the home or in any other group. The former cultivate tendencies in the direction of irresponsibility and gambling, while the latter cultivate the intellect. Having drawn the general line between the games of chance and the games of skill, the former should be checked off at once, as undesirable and dangerous. Card games, with their shuffling and drawing, are typical of the games with a high percentage of chance, though skill is also present. One of America's best-known and greatly-loved evangelists tells of a man who spent twenty-two years in prison because a society woman shamed him into playing a game of cards.

Should it be argued that the chance element is present in the games of skill, it should be answered that there are some games of skill which the Christ way would avoid. Some are too costly in money, or in time, or both. Some of them have an appearance of evil, and should be banned for that reason. But the chance element is reduced in the games of skill, while it is heightened in the games of chance. There is, of course, an element of uncertainty or chance in the commonest and most necessary undertakings of life; but that is a different matter.

The line drawn between the games of chance and those of skill can only be relative, and not a final dividing line between the good and the bad, as the elements of chance and skill appear to be present in all games, but in varying measures. To those who seek the Christ way, the acid test of all play life is the moral and spiritual effect it has upon its devotees. The physical effects are not to be overlooked, for they, too, have a moral bearing, but it is the spiritual which really counts. Is it spiritually helpful to ourselves? Are we helping others in the right way? Does God get glory from it? These are the questions which should be asked and answered in relation to play in which Christians are asked to participate.

It would scarcely seem necessary to mention such recreation as the parlor dance; but since some young people are attracted by it, and are tempted to seek some alibi for it, we must not overlook it.

To the spiritually minded, and to all thoughtful persons, it is evident that the bodily contacts and the suggestive movements of the modern dance are not conducive to pure thoughts and highest morality. It is well known that the parlor dance is the training school for the public dance, and that a very high percentage of fallen women, as well as of degraded men, have reached their low levels by the route of the dance. One does not need to have participated in the dance to know the facts concerning it. The wisest people are those who learn by the experiences of others. The reading of such a book as "From the Ball Room to Hell," by ex-dancing master, T. A. Faulkner, available at almost any religious publishing house, should forever settle the dancing question. The dance is too dangerous a recreation for young life to tamper with, and the Christ way leads straight ahead where the byroad leads aside to this enchanted ground of danger and death.

Legitimate play life in the home makes a positive contribution for good. But beautiful as such play life is, it needs the disciplining hand of wise and sympathetic parenthood to direct it into the Christ way.

Play life in the public schools is absolutely necessary, as everyone knows. There is no reason why the conscientious Christian boy and girl should not engage in the play of the public school, so long as it is conducted in kind and manner consistent with Christian ideals. When play goes beyond that, the Christian student should refrain. Here Christian boys and girls can make a definite contribution to other boys and girls, by engaging in a good and wholesome play life as Christians, refusing to practice anything which would compromise their convictions and high ideals. Even by refusing to participate in anything doubtful they would strengthen themselves in their own Christian lives, and would at the same time become helpful to others.

It is to be regretted that the play life in some public schools, particularly the high school, has been developed away from its original purpose, that of affording physical development and pleasure for the whole group, into that of preparing teams to play against similarly trained teams from other high schools. This is done for the purpose of competition, and upon the pretext of cultivating a school spirit, but the original and proper intent of play life in school has been lost.

Recently, the secretary of the Religious Education Association of one of the mid-Western states, discussing the over-development of play life in the high school, made the remark that one of the largest high schools of his city, the capital of the state, had a gymnasium, but that fourteen students are shut up in it, while fourteen hundred are shut out of it. This is just another way of saying that the play life of the public schools has taken on an unfair, lopsided and regrettable trend, and is badly in need of reform. We should remind ourselves that the way is prepared for the current system of college athletics by the athletic programs of high schools. With inter-school games played by high school children who are wrought up by their leaders to a high pitch of nervous excitement, it is little wonder that college athletics have assumed such proportions.

With the play life of the public schools having already gone to seed in the direction of competitive athletics, it is but a short step to the practice of intercollegiate athletics in the colleges. Here the unnatural forms and over-development continues, and here the objectionable features come more clearly into evidence. Parents who do not desire that their children engage in high-spirited, intercollegiate athletics when they get into college should curb that tendency in them while they are yet in the public schools, or they are likely to insist upon a college for themselves where the athletic spirit is high, or to make trouble for the college which they by force of circumstances must attend, where a moderate play program is maintained.

It is not to be conceded for a moment that play is unnecessary in colleges and similar schools. Anyone who makes such a claim, by that very token confesses that he is either ignorant of the problem of young life shut up to hard and continuous study, or is prejudiced against play itself. In most cases it is the former. There is an occasional institution, attended largely by maturer persons, where industrial employment of various kinds substitutes play almost entirely; but these are the exception, not the rule. The situation is different from that of farm life or other manual labor where work in the open furnishes a sufficient amount of fresh air and exercise. Young people in college are still children, even though of almost mature growth. They still retain the child instinct to play, and that instinct is no less God-given because they have advanced in years and stature. A certain amount of the physical energy of young people who give themselves to study must be worked off in one way or another. If not directed in a legitimate or wholesome way, it is likely to take some undesirable form of activity. It is more than a mere pleasantry to say that, unless students are permitted to work off this excess energy on each other, they are likely to take it out on their professors.

It is not difficult to understand why some prejudices have arisen against play in the institutions of higher learning, when we reckon with what has been developed quite generally in such institutions throughout the land, in the place of a wholesome, helpful play life. This prejudice is illustrated by the following incident. A small Christian college planned to build a gymnasium, the same to be financed by the students and faculty. A good woman of the constituency, evidently prejudiced by what she had known of athletics in other schools, gave herself earnestly to prayer, that something might occur to make the building of the gymnasium impossible. The gymnasium was erected, however, and in that particular institution is used for the housing of the wholesome play life of students. Haunted by fears, lest the history of other institutions should be repeated, this good woman is scarcely to be censured.

The play life in so many institutions, not only those supported by the state, but even church schools, has taken on a form which is being greatly lamented, not merely by the overpious, but by sober-minded educators as well as thoughtful Christians. These have begun to speak out against it, but the thing has grown to such proportions that they are at a loss to know what to do. The situation has not improved since Woodrow Wilson, then President of Princeton University, compared college athletics with "the tail wagging the dog, instead of the dog wagging the tail." If such was the abnormal relation of athletics to college life twenty-five years ago, to what shall we liken it today?

It should be evident to all who think carefully, that the Christ way in the play life of youth discriminates against types of play which are inhuman and destructive, as well as it regulates, and disciplines such types as are human and constructive. There are some games which appear as unchristian from their very nature.

One of the popular high school and college sports has been football. Every year, the football season furnishes a casualty list of from fifteen to thirty deaths, besides the uncounted number of cripples left so for life from the game. This is the price the American peop.e pay in human sacrifice for the privilege of witnessing this brutal game. Neither are these casualties confined to the high schools, as is sometimes contended, but come also from colleges and the Army and Navy Academies. It is difficult to hold a brief for such a sport as this, as it is impossible to find a Christ way in regard to it. It is too sad that progress in relation to necessary things is made sometimes at the cost of life, but who can justify an unnecessary sport at such a price?

In the past so popular has been this sport that he who dared to raise a question concerning it, by that token become unpopular. But within recent years educational boards and school heads have revolted against the sport, with all that accompanies it, and it has been outlawed from a number of Universities.

In the "Literary Digest," issue of January 30, 1932, there appeared an article entitled, "Football Casualties from a Medical Viewpoint." In this article the Journal of the American Medical Association is quoted as follows: "No program of physical culture calls for a mortality record. All the advantages gained through such a game as football should be obtained without loss of life."

The same article quotes Secretary Ray Lyman Wilbur as having said at the White House Conference on Child Health and Protection: "We want to see our children develop into adult citizens with wholesome bodies and prepared minds, both under the control of the developed will operating in the atmosphere of what we call character. * * * We would be able to discover a way by which these aims can be attained without loss of life in our athletic venture."

Recently attempts have been made to revise the game, eliminating from it some of the more dangerous features. But editors contend that, were these features removed, it would no longer be "football," and coaches refuse to eliminate what they call the "spectacular." As Americans we abhor as brutal and uncivilized the Spanish bull fight, but tolerate and even laud a sport right within our midst which levies such a heavy tribute upon human life.

It is so well known that athletics and scholarship are not synonyms that the fact passes as a pleasantry. A young man who attended class in a great university, with a football star of that institution, recently told the writer that when it came the time for this athlete to recite, as if by a common understanding, he was prompted by the various members of the class. This student was one of the idols of the institution, as a member of a team seldom defeated, but was anything but a scholar in his class.

What is the real status of this undesirable something which has superseded the play life in American institutions, this thing so greatly regretted, but which holds institutions in its grip? Summing it up it is this: The legitimate play life has been professionalized, commercialized and corrupted. This abnormal something called athletics is over-developing a few "teams" of bullies at the expense of the physical betterment of the whole group. Thousands of dollars are being expended on the teams, to hundreds spent on all the rest. It demands salaries for highly-trained

athletic coaches, often two or three times the price
paid for regular professorships, and sometimes more
than that received by the presidents of the same institutions. It is laying a heavy money tribute upon
students in order to maintain itself, often compelling
students to discontinue their education because of
the financial strain. It is awakening a gambling spirit,
beginning small but growing rapidly to large proportions. It is sending around over the country, in its
intercollegiate competition, young men and women
who are exposed to the moral hazards of conditions
beyond their control. It has taken on forms so in-
humane, dangerous and brutal that it should not be
permitted in a civilized country; yet it insists upon
being tolerated and even promoted in the name of
Christianity. It demands of its devotees a devotion
so complete as to make everything secondary to it.

Should anyone doubt this delineation of modern
athletics, let him investigate, without prejudice, for
himself. Every one of the above statements could be
extended almost indefinitely, with statistics and facts.
The writer knows whereof he speaks. These are things
which have come under his own observation covering
a number of years of experience. Quite contrary to
the impression given out, not all great men were great
athletes. The sporting world capitalizes whatever it
can find to give out such an impression to young people.

It is coming to be known generally that "athletes
die young." Relative to the corruption of college
athletics, a man who is popular in Y. M. C. A. work,
who himself was a star football player, who came

near losing his life in the game, and who publicly confessed that several splendid physicians had a difficult fight to pull him across the critical period of his life because of his participation in college athletics, recently said: "Unless something is done soon to reform college athletics, within five years it will be as disreputable as the race track." How often have I mingled with young people, in boarding clubs, so frenzied over intercollegiate games that I have had to tolerate baseball, basketball or football for breakfast, dinner and supper! Students in so-called Christian institutions have been known to become so frantically wild over intercollegiate athletics as to do bodily violence to persons who would not participate with them.

Summarizing the whole situation, I have no hesitancy in declaring that the professionalized, commercialized, corrupted athletic system practiced in the majority of institutions of higher learning is not conducive to physical well-being, scholarship, morals or religion. There is no fear of successful refutation. While it is a legitimate thing to train and develop the body if done properly, it must not be done at the expense of the intellectual and spiritual; for "bodily exercise is profitable," but it profiteth but "little" compared to the profit of godliness which "is profitable unto all things." (1 Tim. 4:8.)

What then shall we say? Institutions may count themselves happy where legitimate, healthy, necessary play life has not been superseded by "intercollegiate athletics." Students should consider themselves fortunate, who are privileged to mingle in such play life of a thoroughly Christian institution, and cheerfully assist in maintaining such play life standards. Parents have reasons for genuine gratitude that there are some institutions of higher education where their young people can engage in healthful play, without being exposed to the present system of corrupt athletics. If parents and guardians have becoming interest in the spiritual welfare of their young people, they will discriminate against the institutions where professionalized athletics have been permitted to supersede legitimate and wholesome play life. It is corrupted play, not natural, wholesome play which clashes with piety and holiness.

There is another form of recreation and amusement which sometimes constitutes a serious temptation to Christian young people. It is the theatrical and movie. Little need be said concerning this form of indulgence to such as are Spirit-filled Christians, for they revolt from what is ordinarily on exhibition at such places. Such things as foolishness, crime, illicit love, degradation of the marriage relation and suicide, constitute the usual bill of fare. Spirit-led young people may be momentarily and innocently tempted to such things, but obedience to the Spirit will result in their complete disgust for them. This, again, is a result of the natural play instinct, professionalized, commercialized and corrupted.

Should anyone insist that the movie constitutes "visualized education," let me reply, with Dr. Wm. McKeever, that the commercialized movie industry constitutes a school, but that it is a school of crime. A very high percentage of criminal cases coming before the juvenile courts are directly traceable to this school of crime. It is not against visualized education of a proper and legitimate kind that this conclusion is drawn, but against the commercialized moving-picture industry, with its corrupting tendencies.

Returning, in closing, to the subject of play life more properly, there is no reason why grown-up men and women should not give some attention, in a restricted way of course, to play. They are still children of a larger and more awkward growth, and still possess some of the early instincts. Those who have constant outdoor employment may need no play for the sake of physical exercise. Their only need for play is that of relaxation. Those whose profession requires of them a constant indoor program and mental strain will find play helpful to both body and mind. It affords physical exercise as well as mental relaxation. Teachers do well to engage with their pupils in play, so as to teach them the art of correct and wholesome play. Parents will find it profitable, both for themselves and their children, to engage with them, in the measure opportunity affords, in wholesome, recreational play.

While the problem of the play life is no small one, and very intricate, there is a proper solution of it: there is a Christ way in relation to it. And when that problem is correctly solved, both as to kind and manner, a ban is placed upon the inhuman and destructive, and proper restrictions are placed on the legitimate and best, play will be found not only compatable with the highest good, but to have contributed to the spiritual values of life.

THE CHRIST WAY IN RELATION TO YOUTH'S CHARACTER AND PERSONALITY

Chapter V

THE CHRIST WAY IN RELATION TO YOUTH'S CHARACTER AND PERSONALITY

Character is what one is, while reputation is what one may or may not be. Reputation is the estimate of men, while character is what God knows one to be in his deepest heart motives. Reputation is in the hands of others. Character is in the hands of the individual and his God.

A good name is not to be despised. The writer of Proverbs has said: "A good name is rather to be chosen than great riches." To assume an indifference to reputation and a good name is recklessness and even dangerous. Youth is indebted to family, self, and God to keep a good name.

Just as being is fundamental to doing, so is character to reputation. Deception and counterfeiting are possible to a certain degree, but usually here and now, and certainly hereafter, one's true character is manifest. The searching words of the immortal Lincoln should never be forgotten: "You can fool all of the people a part of the time, and part of the people all the time; but you cannot fool all the people all of the time." To this should be added: "You cannot fool God any of the time."

Being presupposes coming into being. The character which is thoroughly genuine and pure is not obtained in the first birth, but in the second birth, with all that follows. Human nature cannot change its bent and make itself good. One cannot raise himself out of his sinful state any more than he can lift himself over a high fence by his boot straps or shoe laces. He must have saving help apart from himself, and that is just what the Christ way does in human hearts. It is the very genius of Christianity, that it transforms the bad heart into the good. The Christ way in us makes possible the Christ way through us.

Youth faces no more serious responsibility than to attend to the matter of character. This suggestion carries with it the assumption that if the matter of character is properly attended to, a good reputation will also follow.

While the crises of the Christian life bring the heart into the proper character attitude, character itself is a thing of growth. The quality of character will be largely determined by the thought life, for the texture of character is woven by the threads of our thinking. "As he thinketh within himself, so is he" (Proverbs 23:7) was not only true centuries ago, but remains true always.

Breaks of character sometimes appear to come suddenly, but such is not the case. Long before the visible break there had been woven into the fabric, though unseen, a weak series of threads, and under the severe test the crash resulted.

Many a young man and woman who had never before stepped aside, even in the smallest measure, in conduct, and had never been suspected of weakness, capitulated under subtle temptation and fell because there was a weakness in character due to a secret thought attitude of a compromising nature. Unconsciously, to them, they had been weakened and made susceptible to that particular temptation.

Young men and women who are strong in character, and are able to resist temptations of the most subtle kind, are those who guard their secret thought attitudes against evil as jealously as they guard their open conduct. Such will not be found off guard when subtle temptation confronts them. Such an one was Joseph, one of the most faultless of Old Testament characters.

The following story is told of a railroad engineer who ran his passenger train through the Allegheny mountains. The railroad was double tracked, and some of the grades were very steep. He had frequently seen empty freight cars crushed on the downward grade, by the heavy train of cars back of them, and thus made to "buckle," extending out over the other railroad track, and seriously endangering other trains and human lives should the passing train meet the one with the "buckled" car. He had pondered over the matter many a time. What would he do should he meet a freight train with a "buckled" car? His engine might be thrown from the track, together with the cars attached, and the whole load of precious human freight dashed to death over the deep and precipitous embankment. This was what he decided upon: Should he ever meet a situation as described, he would throw open the throttle of his engine, strike the obstacle in its path as hard as possible, thus tossing it aside and clearing the rails for his engine and the train.

Years passed by, and no emergency of this kind arose.

But the decision was definite, positive and fixed. He knew his attitude to such a danger and reviewed it a thousand times. There was no question, no indecision, no hesitancy. One day, when danger seemed as far away as it ever could be, while rounding one of those sharp curves with his load of passengers, this engineer saw coming toward him a freight train with a buckled car. The car extended to the side, practically covering the track ahead of him. Instantly he opened wide the throttle of his engine, struck the box car with an increasing speed, and tossed it out of the way. He then stopped his train, every wheel upon the tracks and every one of the hundreds of passengers safe. When asked the secret of his unusual feat, the engineer told the story as given here. His decision had been made and fixed in advance, and saved the dangerous situation.

When this story is transferred into the realm of character, it is easy to see how the thought life makes or breaks in the moment of sudden and subtle moral danger.

Character is closely related to personality, for the latter embraces the former, though it includes more and is more tangible than character. Personality is character plus.

Personality is the only thing which is absolutely one's own. Whether added to or subtracted from, it still remains one's own. A fine personality is an asset impossible to evaluate, and a prize worthy of greatest emulation.

Not all possess an attractive personality, although such appears to be the heritage of some. But whether it is an imposing personality, an average, or even a subnormal one, that personality is ours, and we, as individuals, are compelled to wear that personality, wherever we are and go, for a lifetime. It is, like our shadow, ever present. In the light of this fact, whether it be a welcome or an unwelcome one, it becomes self-evident that the subject of personality outweighs every other one.

But personality is not a matter of the body only. Personality is a dichotomy—includes the physical and the spiritual. The former is the material aspect of personality, that part which is ever in evidence, while the spirit is the immaterial, which functions through the visible body. It is folly to discuss which is the more important as they relate to personality, the body or the spirit, for as we know personality it necessarily includes both.

It is a natural ambition, then, and by no means an unworthy one, to develop our God-given personalities to the highest point of efficiency possible. Perhaps it should be stated still more strongly, that God has entrusted us with what we call personality, and that it is our religious duty to guard and to develop that personality to its maximum of strength and usefulness for His own glory. God is interested in personalities more than in anything else in the world, for it is in this realm that He more nearly reflects Himself to the world. It is here where God comes nearest unveiling His countenance to men. If He is not seen and recognized here, He is seen and recognized nowhere.

It is to be insisted, then, that whatever our natural heritage by way of personality, that personality may be added to or subtracted from, in no small measure. Though man was created holy, and in the image of God, sin has through the fall left its marks upon both soul and body. For the removal of the effects of sin upon the soul, provision has been made in the present, full salvation. For the complete removal of the marks of the fall from the body, a glorious resurrection awaits. In the meantime, it becomes the spirit, the major member of this dichotomy of personality, to make the best of its trust, and to attend to the matter of personality in the way which will reflect greatest glory upon its Maker.

It is as though God had made man the architect of his own personality—a difficult task.   To take into one's hand the mallet and chisel and turn sculptor to a block of marble or stone, or to paint with brush upon canvas, is an easy task compared with the architecture of personality. The former is objective; the latter is subjective, rendering the task more difficult.

The Christ way makes for an improved personality. It would be amusing, were it not for the pathos, to observe how certain ones set themselves to the task of self-improvement. Often it is attempted by the use of cosmetics and all sorts of external appliances and trappings. Such an attempt is, first of all, an indictment against the personal appearance of the individual who makes it, and is certain to cheapen personality rather than enrich it.

Personality has its visible and physical marks, but cannot be donned externally. Improvement of personality is the result of a cause which lies deep—as deep as the inner motives of the heart. The securing of a pure heart, which results in a clean, consistent outward life, is at once an improvement of the inner personality, the soul, and the placing into the hand of the soul an instrument for external improvement. If it be unclean, of untidy clothing, an unwashen face and unkempt hair, the Christ way will prescribe clean and becoming clothes, water, soap, towel and comb. If, perchance, there is the conspicuous absence of beauty, a pure heart is most certain to reflect itself upon the countenance which is the index of the soul, and enhance its features.

With the many handicaps of the race relative to physical form and feature, beauty is not within the reach of all. But beauty which comes as the result of pure hearts is one which cannot be marred by passing incident or washed off by tears or raindrops. True, not all can be large and robust; not all can be fair and beautiful, or handsome; but all may share in the benefits of personal improvement which comes as the result of pure hearts.

There is no reason why Christ's people should not be the most attractive people in all the world—the most beautiful women and the most handsome men. The holy young men in Babylon, Daniel and his three Hebrew friends, were found not only ten times better in wisdom and understanding than the magicians and enchanters, but were fairer and fatter than all the youths which did eat of the king's dainties.

To determine whether or not purity of heart and life improves personality, one only needs to observe the results which are obtained when a sinner comes to Christ. Repeatedly has it occurred, particularly in city missions, that such who came to the altar of prayer and found Christ were scarcely recognizable when they returned to the next service. The consistent dress, the changed attitude toward the bodily appearance, the transformed countenance—the whole outer personality—testified to the inner change which had worked wonders externally.

Dr. Torrey tells of a young Christian woman who was a member of the Bible Institute with which he was connected. As every Institute member was required to go out among the poor, and seek to lead them to Christ, this girl was engaged on a certain day doing this kind of work. The Spirit of the Lord was striving with her relative to consecration, which apparently involved missionary work in South Africa; but she was stoutly resisting. On this particular day, as she walked along the Lake Shore drive, in Chicago, she noted the beautiful homes along its course. "Ah!" she said to herself, "this is what I like; I have had enough of dirty old stairways and squalor!" She had been fighting against the Holy Spirit, but deep in her heart she was gradually yielding to His leadings. At the supper table that evening, he says, "The Holy Ghost and fire fell upon her. In an instant she ran across the room, threw her arms around a girl friend who was staying with her, and exclaimed, 'I'm a volunteer for South Africa.'" The fire of the Lord had burnt up everything evil in her heart and life. So transformed was she henceforth in her views, purposes, ambitions —nay, in her very face—that her best and closest friends could hardly believe she was the same girl.

There is scripture warrant for insisting that right

relation with God is reflected advantageously upon the countenance of its possessor. The Preacher of Ecclesiastes says: "A man's wisdom maketh his face to shine, and the hardness of his face is changed."—Eccl. 8:1. The Psalmist also declared: "For Jehovah taketh pleasure in his people; he will beautify the meek with salvation."—Psa. 149:4. Imagine, if you can, the Christian, from whose face radiates the joy and glory of right relation with God, whom He has beautified with salvation, attempting to fix up outward personality by questionable methods and artificial trappings! Such things as these would make the child of God look cheap and trashy.

The Christ way does not destroy individualities.

There are no two persons alike. Scientists tell us that there are no two blades of grass or two leaves on the trees alike. Of the billions of snow crystals which fall in winter, we are told, no two are alike. They may appear to the casual observer as alike, but when submitted to microscopic examination, are found to be very different. Twins who appear to resemble each other greatly are found to possess differences which make them sufficiently individualistic. Variety is the spice of life. God wanted no two people alike. The God who created man was great and wise enough to make no replicas.

The Christ way does not destroy personal likes and dislikes when no moral is involved.

Consistent with personal individuality are personal tastes. In the matter of dress, one may prefer a particular color or a particular shape. Even within the limits of colors and styles acceptable to the most conscientious Christians, there is a great variety from which individual taste may select. Groups of people are at liberty to agree upon these matters, and practice uniformity if they so elect, but it is folly to attempt to destroy individual tastes in relation to these things.

The matter of personal choice enters into occupations. Eliminating any questionable occupations and professions, there is still a range wide enough to meet the preferences of saved men and women. The wisdom of personal preference is easily seen in the matter of occupations, for a variety of workers is needed to meet the needs of society. No thoughtful person would desire the destruction of personal preference in the matter of kinds of work.

In the matter of eating, personal taste figures largely. Without reckoning with harmful things by way of meat and drink, there is a vast field for the varieties of taste. There are some things perfectly nutritious and valuable for food to which one has a positive aversion, while, on the other hand, there are things of which he is decidedly fond. Purity of heart does not change these legitimate tastes.

The Christ way does not destroy peculiarities of habits, or even of speech.

Perhaps nothing is more undesirable than conscious or unconscious copying of the habits and movements of others. Misfits are the rule when people attempt to be what they are not—someone else. Not a few have made themselves ridiculous in this way. In vocabulary, Paul differed from John, and Luke differed from both. David, Jeremiah and Ezekiel differed in their reactions to the revelation of God. David was frequent in praise, with his characteristic expression, "Praise ye the Lord." Jeremiah was the weeping prophet, with eyes as "fountains of tears." Ezekiel was the man of "visions," always seeing marvelous things. God employs different tools with which to carry on His work. Though God would not have us to be eccentric, He sometimes capitalizes the peculiarities of His workmen and uses them. He wants us to be ourselves—our very best selves—though that may mean to be different from all others, in some respects.

The human make-up is so diverse that there is no uniform manner by which people demonstrate their joys and sorrows. Sorrow opens a floodgate to some hearts, while to others it consumes even the tears. Joy finds its expression in some lives by laughter, clapping of the hands or other outward demonstration, while in other instances it calls forth a tear and produces a sinking into quiet relaxation.

A veteran of the Civil War once related the reactions which he witnessed in his brigade at the announcement of the close of the war. General Kiefer was in command. For days there had been rumors that the war had probably reached the end. One day General Kiefer was observed coming in the distance, riding his horse as fast as it could run. As he came nearer it could be seen that his horse was white with the lather of sweat, and was almost exhausted. All eyes were turned, and ears were turned expectantly. When the general came close enough, he arose in his saddle and exclaimed: "The war is over." And such a demonstration! Some of the men shouted; some tossed their hats high in the air; some broke down and wept in silent tears; some actually threw themselves upon the ground and rolled in the dust. The announcement meant the same thing to all. Hostilities were over; guns might be stacked and swords sheathed; they might all return home to friends and loved ones. But the variety of demonstration was in keeping with the variety of personality.

The Christ way does not destroy, but should assist in developing the aesthetic nature—the love of the beautiful.

There is nothing in the Christ way which forbids the love of the truly beautiful. It is a self-appointed and vicious authority which seeks to minister a severe crushing to one of the most natural and desirable instincts of youthful hearts. As if the beautiful must, of necessity, be unholy, something of a taboo has been placed upon everything beautiful.

"The heavens declare the glory of God," declares the Psalmist. God is the Author of holiness and the Father of holy people. Whose prerogative is it, to forbid God's child from viewing the heavens with its stars of the first and lesser magnitudes, observing the golden band of the "milky way" and the arrangement of the constellation groups, with a sense of inexpressible ecstasy, because it is his Father whose glory is being declared? Why should God's child be less appreciative of the unfolding bud, the stretch of green landscape, the rippling brook, the breath of flowers, the singing of the birds, the rendering of a great oratorio, a discovery or fact of science, a glorious sunrise or an equally glorious sunset? What is there in a close relationship to God which should or does destroy the appreciation of beauty in things which He has made?

On the other hand, the Christ way gives a sense and appreciation of the beautiful things which God has made and which He sustains, which cannot be experienced by such as know not God as Father.

Some years ago the writer was the young pastor of a splendid though small parish in a mid-Western state. His father-in-law, also a minister, but of maturer experience, was visiting in his home when a distant member of the congregation arrived, driving an outfit more rickety than he is here willing to describe. The poor, lame horse, the topless, cushion-torn buggy with its loose spokes and rattling tires, presented a sorry spectacle. After the noon meal when the visitor desired to depart, with a courtesy becoming Christian hospitality, the horse was hitched and driven to the front gate, where the father-in-law had arrived a few moments in advance of the owner of the outfit. With a sense of conscious shame, the writer remarked: "If I had to drive this outfit, I should have to pray for more grace." After a moment of silence, a reply came from the father-in-law which has never been forgotten. It conveyed a philosophy often overlooked, and even ignored. This was the answer: "Yes, and perhaps the more grace you would get, the less you would want to drive such an outfit." Indeed, grace does not destroy, but enhances the appreciation of the beautiful. If properly instructed, it will develop the aesthetic nature in a way so as to make it not only a delightful but valuable asset.

In the development of the aesthetic nature the Christ

way insists upon discrimination. It is unalterably opposed to pretense and the hypocritical. Whether it be the artificial and forbidden trapping in an effort to adorn the outward, such as "gold, pearls or costly array," the affectation of the personality of another, the veneer and whitewash of an insincere etiquette, to these things the Christ way is always and everywhere opposed.

The Christ way exhibits a decided aversion to things which are less than genuine—the make-believe.

The writer was invited, not long since, to deliver the address to a Sunday School Teachers' graduating class. Upon entering the church his eyes fell upon a remarkable profusion of foliage and flowers. An arch entwined with wisteria encircled the pulpit. Great pots of roses and peonies, as large as saucers, sat on either side of the speaker's stand. On the piano was a vase of lilies, while around the desk a honeysuckle twined in full bloom. Imagine the peculiar sensation experienced by the speaker, when he discovered that the whole profusion was artificial. Not a genuine leaf, bud or flower was in evidence. He does not charge that people as having symbolized their religion by the array of the make-believe in floral display, but frankly confesses that a single, fragrant, unfolding, sure-enough flower would have been appreciated infinitely more by him than all the overdone exhibit of the artificial. Above everything else, Christ desires the genuine in everything.

Then lastly, the Christ way seeks to set the beautiful in proper relation to the true and the good. Even beautiful things can be overdone, to the neglect of the things which may not necessarily come within the category of the beautiful. The aesthetic nature may be developed to abnormal proportions; but there is nothing so certain to develop the individual personality so proportionately as purity of heart. It knows how, and can subordinate all else to the true and good. It can go further than that: It knows that all that is true and good is beautiful, and that all that is beautiful is true and good. A right attitude and relation to God makes possible the proper coordination and relation of all things in life which are worthwhile.

It is sin which has made man unnatural. The Christ way restores to one's real and most natural self—nearest to what God made him and desires him to be. The Christ way would have saved millions of young men and women from early death and premature graves. It is most certainly saving millions from such an undesirable fate. It improves personality, does not destroy individuality, but cultivates the best things in human hearts to the glory of the Creator and the decided advantage of its devotees.

THE CHRIST WAY IN YOUTH'S SOCIAL RELATIONSHIPS

Chapter VI

THE CHRIST WAY IN YOUTH'S SOCIAL
RELATIONSHIPS

Man is a social being. God made him so, for He
wanted him to be such. "It is not good that man
should be alone," is one of the earliest decrees of
God. "I will make a help-meet for him," was
God's solution of the primary social problem. The
first man recognized woman as, bone of his bones, and
flesh of his flesh, constituting them "one flesh." The
sexes thus complement each other, in keeping with the
Divine wisdom and plan.

The social current, then, cannot but run the deepest,
except that of religion, and these two are inseparable.
It was because of this fact that a woman said of Jesus that He told her all that she ever did, when
He made a single statement about her social affairs.

Since the social relationship is so fundamental and
so determining in regard to everything, it is reasonable to conclude that there must be a Christ way in
regard to it, if there is a Christ way in relation to
anything. It is on this point that youth needs its
fullest enlightenment. Some other things in relation
to life may be corrected, but a social blunder is almost, or altogether, irreparable. The subject takes
on seriousness and nobility in proportion to its importance.

This is indeed a subject in which every normal

young person is interested, whether he is anxious to confess it or not. It is perfectly legitimate, and the writer invites the young reader to enter with him into the discussion, assured that no confidence will be betrayed, and that no sacred matter will be treated lightly.

The social instinct asserts itself early, and appears first in the play life. The tiny girl with her doll, or family of dolls, is beautifully and innocently giving expression to the social instinct of her being which is woven into the very fabric of her existence. The little boy and girl engaged in the play of housekeeping are running true to the laws of their social being. This social instinct is their common heritage, and when environed in the way that children are expected to be, it is only natural that they should be socially inclined.

With the dawning of the adolescence the social instinct asserts itself more strongly, and somewhere near, or soon after, the middle teens, sometimes becomes, in normal youth, a veritable social upheaval. It is that period when youth fails to understand itself; when passion surges ahead of judgment. This period is a trying one for all concerned, for both youth and parents or guardians. It is sometimes unsympathetically dubbed the period of "puppy love." It is the period when sympathetic interest and enlightenment is sorely needed; when a patient but firm and steadying hand is imperative. Blundering at this period has resulted in the shipwreck of many lives. In many cases, even where life has not been completely wrecked, handicaps of lifetime seriousness have resulted from hasty and unwise decisions made in this period of social upheaval.

For every one of the social contacts there is the Christ way, and the discovery of this way should be the sincere and prayerful quest of every Christian youth. The Christ way will be found to be the way of the well-guarded social contacts.

What should we expect the Christ way to be in relation to the less formal groups or gatherings? What should be the conversation and conduct of a group of young people meeting together informally? It is this type of a gathering where a subtle temptation sometimes lurks. Were the occasion a formal one, opportunity would have been afforded for discrimination in advance. The Christ way refuses participation in anything, whether conduct or conversation, which lowers or even tends to lower the standards of thoroughly Christian conduct, or in the smallest way compromises grace and virtue.

Waiving everything else of a more questionable nature, conversation sometimes takes, unintentionally, an unchristlike trend. Where is the young person who has not had an experience similar to this? A group of young people were together. There was not uttered a suggestive word, much less one of obscenity or profanity. But the conversation assumed a light, meaningless, or trashy character. One light thing was innocently said, which provoked another of a similar nature, and thus the conversation was started and ran. When the young people separated and went to their homes, some of them discovered a painful emptiness which resulted from a slightly unguarded informal gathering. The joy and sweetness of soul had ebbed out, as a result of light and meaningless conversation.

It is not intended that a ban should be placed upon cheerful, pleasant and purposeful words. These are necessary and desirable. They are the idle or empty words for which we must give an account (Matt. 12: 36), and which rob us of our joy and peace, and against which we are cautioned.

There is also a Christ way in relation to the smaller social groups.

If it is imperative that the Christ way be found in relation to the larger group, it is equally, and possibly more so, that it be discovered in relation to the smaller social group, when the company becomes more select. It is characteristic of social relations that they trend from the larger circle to the smaller, with an increasing and intensifying interest.

That one is known by the company he keeps, is a familiar adage, and one which few seek to refute. The good and the bad, the holy and the unholy, do not mix any better than do oil and water. He who seeks to fool others in this matter is himself most fooled. Christians must touch others in some way, if they would seek to win them to Christ, but they cannot afford to enter into questionable social companionship with them to do so. Too many sad experiences are upon record of those who, upon the pretext of hoping to win others, have exposed themselves to questionable contacts, only to discover later that they had overestimated their own spiritual strength, and had failed. "Birds of a feather flock together" is still true. The contacts which young people should make, with a view of saving others, should be in the broader circle, and not within the smaller social range. The handicap is too great, and the risk is too serious. God does not require it of youth, thus to expose itself.

Then, may we inquire, What is the Christ way in relation to the smallest social group—the most select, the two-by-two group?

It is an interesting thing to note how the social instinct continues its process of elimination. Once it was content with the larger group, in which there were many friendships of equal evaluation. Gradually the range lessened, embracing a smaller number. Of course, the other and larger circle of friendships continued, but it no longer met the exacting demands of the social instinct. By an inexplicable process the circle was narrowed until it reached this group—that of the two-by-two.

Assuming that the Christ way has been pursued, and that discrimination has been most exacting, in keeping with the Christ way we shall expect to find in this holy of holies of the smallest social group two persons of kindred spirits—two Christ's ones, for they have followed the Christ way.

If there is one place where, above others, the Christ way should have been pursued, it is here. It is here that life companionships are contracted; where futures are determined which involve the coming generations. The happiness of two and the well-being of others are in the balance in this smallest of social groups. Even eternal destinies are at stake.

It is one of the strangest of things that some young people are so indifferent to all that is involved in their choices of life companionship. Heedless of their own better judgment, the advice of parents, friends and pastors, they persist in friendships, and finally enter into marriage covenants which are certain, or almost so, to bring them lifelong unhappiness.

How a Christian young person can enter into fellowship with a non-Christian, and expect to be happy and successful, is difficult to understand. Certainly the social relationships, especially when they are reduced to the smaller group, are comprehended in Paul's great preachment and question when he said: "Be not unequally yoked with unbelievers: for what fellowship have righteousness and iniquity? or what communion hath light with darkness? And what concord hath Christ with Belial? or what portion hath a believer with an unbeliever?"—2 Cor. 6:14, 15. "Marrying a man to reform him," is the folly in which many a more worthy woman has sorrowingly and in vain spent her life. An ounce of social prevention is worth a ton of cure. The pure, the noble and the virtuous have a right to insist upon the same qualities in others who seek to enter their smaller and smallest social groups. Nay, more, they owe it to themselves, to their Christ, and all others who are worthy, to be uncompromising in regards to this matter.

Young people should choose friendships with those whose past records are known, and whose character has been tested and proven. This is a day of shams, and there is no place where the make-believe is more to be sought out and eliminated than in friendships. A counterfeit dollar is worthless, and may be discarded, but counterfeit companions are a living grief. It is not enough that a young person professes to be a Christian, to merit the faith of another worthy Christian young person. Confidence should be established through a period of years of upright, virtuous living, so that there need be no fears as to character.

It is particularly true of pure young women, that they have been made the prey of young men who feigned religion that they might secure their friendship, and their hands in hasty marriage. So often has this occurred that young women need to be reminded of the danger which lurks in friendships with those of unknown and doubtful pasts. In pointing out this peril, no reflection is intended against any worthy person. But in cases where the record is clean and satisfactory, there is no fear of the light. Beware of those who insist upon covered records. Over against this dark and pessimistic suggestion, there is a more optimistic one, which is, that there are still many young men who are worthy of the friendships of pure and beautiful young women.

While lingering about the matter of social choices, let us remind ourselves that not every good person will make another happy. Suitability, adaptability and taste should play their parts. The Christ way always leads to the good, but does not ignore the things which contribute to happiness and success. The Christ way concerning marriage is that it is a life relationship, therefore, by the same token should be approached most thoughtfully and prayerfully.

We have blundered in assuming, up to this point, that the smallest social group is composed of only two. According to the Christ way, there are no unchaperoned, two-by-two groups. There is always a third, invited party, whose presence adds pleasure and enhances happiness. In keeping with the requirements of those who are responsible for young people in their social relationships, the chaperone is a necessity, but often unwelcome. It is Christ, Himself, who comes into this, the smallest of social groups, when He is invited, and it is He who becomes the third party.

When the proper social relationships obtain, there is sweet communion between these three. Not only do the two fellowship together, but they fellowship together with Him. This is a good practice, and merits commendation. There is upon record the account of the social relationships of a young man and woman who became life partners, happy parents, honored citizens, and who distinguished themselves in Christian service, who made it a practice to welcome the Third Person into their smallest social group. It is said that they never spent an evening together, in which they did not spend some time upon their knees, communing with their welcome guest. Social relationships pursued after this manner are worthy of emulation, and there should be no surprise if they result in happy homes and successful lives.

It scarcely needs be said that young people who take Christ with them into their smallest social groups, will become keenly conscious of the fact that their bodies are the temples of the Holy Spirit (1 Cor. 6:19), and will conduct themselves in the matters of their courtship accordingly. These body-temples will be carefully and consistently clothed. Anything which would mar the beauty and despoil the purity of unsullied soul will be banned. There will be a definitely-fixed and well-understood opposition, on the part of both persons, against turning a beautiful, legitimate, Christian courtship into petting parties of doubtful consequence at their best, and ofttimes of serious outcome. Someone has said that the petal of the white rose or lily is never so beautiful after being man-handled. Young people will be greatly rewarded for having maintained the very highest Christian ideals in their most intimate social attachments. For their own sakes, for the sakes of those whom they love, and for the sakes of their future offspring, they can well afford to practice the Christ way, heeding the admonition once given to a young man: "Keep thyself pure." —1 Tim. 5:22.

If only youth would take seriously the advice to wear the social cloak loosely, and to take plenty of time to approach and decide the matter of life companionship, they would save themselves a great deal of trouble, and many lives would be more happy and successful. Many a useful career has been spoiled by a too early marriage, which has made it impossible to complete the preparation for the work of life. Often college students, and sometimes young people of high school age, become socially impatient, making themselves believe the false adage, that "two can live cheaper than one," and are married. They hope to continue their education, only to be disillusioned later. In nearly every such case at least one of the contracting parties never returns to school, and, in many instances, neither is able to do so. Life becomes constantly more complex, and promising lives are permanently handicapped.

There is another extreme to be avoided—that of indifference to marriage, but against this only a few young people need to be cautioned. A reasonably early marriage is more natural and ideal, but the preparation for life which requires all the energies, time and resources of young people for several years, should be completed before marriage. This is decidedly to the advantage of both parties, their future families, and to the work to which they are led.

There is no intention to conceal the fact that the Christ way in social relationships leads normally to marriage. It is here that the social aspect of life makes its highest reach, and to which everything else is incidental and tributary. Here one man and one woman become one flesh. It is here that the greatest determining human factor in the destinies of men and nations, the home, is established. The decision of God which placed Abraham at the head of the chosen nation was based upon the family relationship. God knew that he would "command his children and his household after him." (Gen. 18:19.) There may have been other men as good as Abraham in many things, and possibly in a few things superior, but it was this family idealism which determined God's choice. How important that the home be established in the truly Christian way!

May it not be that herein lies the reason for the subtle and incessant attack against the home? The grind of the divorce mill is a sad commentary upon the sacred institution of marriage. The increase in divorces in the United States is alarming. In the year 1887 there occurred 27,919 divorces. Forty years later, in 1927, there were granted 192,037 divorces, slightly more than seven times the number of divorces granted in 1887. The number had increased in 1928 to 195,939, and in 1929 to 201,475. In 1909 there were 8.9 divorces granted for every one hundred marriages. In the year 1919, ten years later, the number had increased to 12.3 divorces for every one hundred marriages, and in 1929 to 16.3. These figures show that in 1929, approximately every sixth marriage in the United States was set aside by divorce. The average of 16.3 divorces for every one hundred marriages is obtained by averaging the divorce rate in the various states, which ranged from the highest which was Nevada, where there occurred one divorce for every 2.3 marriages, to New York State, the lowest, where a divorce occurred for every 23.6 marriages. The other states of the Union vary between these two figures.

If these figures are correct, and they probably are, as they have been taken from the New Standard Encyclopedia, a very sad state of affairs exists in this great country of ours in relation to marriage and the home. It is a situation which should challenge youth. Divorce is a terrible thing, bringing with it grievous complications irreparable. It is almost impossible to extricate those who are caught in its snare, so that there is little prospect for those included in a statistic like this given here. Our only hope lies with the young, to whom we trust to be able to bring some help, by keeping them out of the grind of the divorce court and the certain evils of divorce.

It is true that the causes for the divorce situation in the United States lie upon the very surface of things. The marriage is prostituted in theatrical performances and in moving pictures; is treated as a huge joke from many platforms and in many magazines; and too often spoken of lightly even from pulpits. There is one cause, however, which lies back of the whole distressing situation: it is the failure to take the Christ way in the social relationships. The only hope for the rising generation, and remedy for this evil, then, is the Christ way, to which we lovingly invite our youth. Surely Christian young people will not fail to heed the counsel and admonition.

The marriage relationship properly approached and sacredly kept is one of the most beautiful things in the world. For two Christian young people to give themselves wholly to each other for life is at once heroic and sacred. It is true that the road which lies ahead is unknown to them, but it is not unknown to Him into whose hand they both place theirs, if the Christ way is taken in marriage. To such marriage is not lottery, but an assured success. To such it will be a never-ending pleasure to keep the vows made on that eventful day: "To love, honor and keep, in days of good and evil report, in sickness and health, in poverty and wealth, and, forsaking all others, keep themselves only unto each other until death doth separate them."

Homes established by those who approach and consummate marriage in the Christ way will be established genuinely Christian, and it is a very high probability that these homes will be maintained as such. This is, indeed, one of the greatest needs of the church and the nation—Christian homes.

It is also assumed that marriage and the establishment of homes in the Christ way will result in the rearing of sons and daughters for Christ and His kingdom. Children are naturally-expected and divinely-planned fruitage of the marriage relation. Young people who are unwilling to assume the parental responsibility have no right to marry. Homes without children, purposely so, should be condemned, while childless homes, unavoidably such, should be pitied. No married pair has paid its racial debt until two children have been reared, and it is only beyond the rearing of two that any contribution to the race is made. But this debt is not merely racial, it is owed to God, for it is God who commanded such who enter the marriage state: "Be ye fruitful." (Gen. 1:28.)

Parenthood is a relation so unique and wonderful that the thoughtful and natural do not wish to escape it. Receiving into parental arms, and looking into faces of tiny bits of humanity fashioned of one's own flesh and blood afford a thrill unlike any other in human experience. The rearing of children, the supplying of their needs, their nurture and their discipline brings out and develops the finest and best in human nature. Then, to realize that this is the Divine plan that God should be glorified in our social relationship, challenges every young man and woman to seek the Christ way in relation to all of these things, lest God should fail of His glory and life's greatest happiness and success should be missed.

THE CHRIST WAY IN YOUTH'S VOCATIONS

Chapter VII

THE CHRIST WAY IN YOUTH'S VOCATIONS

God's first interest in young life is in relation to its being, and second only to that is His interest in its doing.

It ought not to be a difficult matter to see the very close and vital relation between the Christ way and life vocations. But this relation is more vital than is supposed by such as give it only a superficial consideration.

It is perfectly natural and legitimate that the question of life vocations be raised very early. The little boy and girl raise the question very soon, in the terms of play, and sometimes in word. The child who does not do this is not normal. My own little lad, not more than five or six years of age, once said to me: "Papa, could a person be a band-man and a preacher, both?" It is easily seen that this little child was already raising the question of a life vocation, and the struggle between being a musician and a minister had assumed such proportions in his little mind that he was seeking a compromise between the two, at that early age. Of course, it was not to be assumed, necessarily, that he would become either, as a result of this childish struggle. He did become a minister, however, and his experience illustrates the fact that the problem of life vocations is one which presents itself very early in the life of a normal child.

As young people grow older, the problem of life vocations becomes more serious and real. The high school age, the age of adolescence, is likely to bring a brief period of vocational upheaval, corresponding to the social upheaval of that age. It is at this period that the high school boy comes home from school one day, and, throwing aside his books, informs his parents that he must quit school and get a "job" at once. Many parents have proved themselves weak at this moment, and concurred in the wish of the son which was stimulated by this vocational tempest, both to their regret and that of the boy. Here again, wise, sympathetic and firm guidance is necessary on the part of the parents or guardian.

Gradually the subject of life vocations takes on a seriousness and more reasonable form, as the college age is reached. To the young person of these years, the matter is, or at least should be, a very important one, and should be given most thoughtful and devotional consideration.

There is need for sanctified young men and women in all the legitimate relationships, occupations, professions and callings.

Take, to begin with, the home relationship—that relationship which is all-inclusive of every occupation, profession and calling. The home relationships, those of husband, wife, father and mother, are more vital to the church, and state, than all else combined. It is the home which is the foundation of church and state, and when once the Christian home is gone, "Ichabod" may well be written upon the banners of both, for the glory has already departed. So, first of all, holy young men and women are needed to fill these relationships.

Then there are the necessary occupations of life. Of these there are all kinds—a variety so great and diversified as to suit the human tastes and talents, from the tilling of the soil to the management of vast industries. In every one of these necessary occupations there is plenty of room for the fully-consecrated Christian. What a blessing it would be to these vocations, and through them to the world, if there should enter the ranks a host of young people who would engage in them for the glory of God, and with His conscious blessing upon them! The thought of the possibility of farming for the Lord, of conducting a business enterprise with Him as the Big Partner, or the managing of a vast industry in the same spirit and with the same motive, should thrill young people to their finger tips. But whether it be any of these named, or any other good and necessary occupation, it is possible to engage in it for the glory of God.

Then, there are the legitimate professions from which sanctified young people are not excluded. Perhaps I should say that such have a peculiar qualification for these professions.

The profession of teaching affords an opportunity for making a worthwhile contribution to the oncoming generation, second, possibly, only to that of the sacred callings. Realizing the tremendous potentialities of young life, and recalling the plasticity of boyhood and girlhood, it is difficult to refrain from praying and hoping that God would lay His hand upon an increasingly large number of young people from thoroughly Christian homes, who themselves are in the experience

of full salvation, and lead them to the necessary training for public school teaching, and thus fill up the
ranks of grade and high school teachers. The teaching profession may be "underpaid," but there are com-
pensations for the work of teaching apart from the
pay checks received. Many of the states give the Bible
some place in the public schools, and none of them ex-
clude the incarnation of its teachings in the form of
a person. Wonderful opportunities are here!

There is the profession of medicine—a profession
with wonderful opportunity for good—but so largely
manned with those who have lost themselves in the
purely materialistic, and have become skeptical or
indifferent, or, if Christians at all, only nominally
so. This is certainly to be regretted, and there is, beyond doubt, a great need for well saved and thoroughly
consecrated young men in this profession, to bring to
it and to suffering humanity a ministry as only such
can bring.

The writer is delighted to say that there are, among
his intimate friends, several physicians of this type,
who have brought to this profession the higher motive
which impels consecrated souls, and have an interest
in their patients which reaches beyond their physical
well-being. These good men pray for their patients, and
sometimes with them. Often they send around to the
bedside of a spiritually needy patient some pastor or
preacher, whose direct duty it becomes to offer a soul
ministry.

Then, there is the profession of nursing, which offers
such a wonderful opportunity. It is a beautiful ministry, and bears a very close relation to the sacred call-

ings. Whenever I meet a young woman who says that she has decided to or has taken up the work of nursing, she receives my congratulations and blessing; for I am almost certain that she has been impelled by motives high and humane, perhaps holy. She merits encouragement and approval.

Time forbids an enumeration of the other professions into which Christ way young people may enter, even after careful discrimination is made against unworthy professions. But one needs not to go outside of the legitimate and worthy pursuits of life to find challenges enough for the brainiest of brain and the brawniest of brawn. Wonderful challenges to young men and women!

The Christ way leads young people to their various places in life. Unless we are led by the Spirit in relation to our life vocations we will be left to our incompetent and shortsighted judgment, and are likely to choose selfishly or drift with the varying circumstances.

There is only one place for each to fill in life, but there is one place for each. God has a distinct plan for our lives, no matter who we are, what our names, where we live, what our circumstances, how much or how little we know, provided we are willing to accept His plan. No one is so important and so favorably situated, nor so insignificant and handicapped, as to have escaped His notice and plan.

Then, too, God's plans for our various lives are infinitely bigger and better than we could ever have dreamed out for ourselves. This should be good news for all, but particularly for those who are conscious of some measure of handicap. See this picture: A little lad face to face with the handicap of near-poverty, a member of a large family, compelled to work among strangers from the age of twelve, obliged to have his school years cut short at both ends by autumn and spring work,—deprived of many of the privileges accorded to the average youth of today. Now see the picture: A man in early middle life, who is known as a minister, an editor, author, teacher, lecturer and educator, with a demand for his services far beyond his time and ability to meet. What is the secret of such a career, despite the original handicap? It is this: Self plans were abandoned and surrendered, and in exchange the bigger, richer and better plan of God was accepted. God's plans are not the same for each life; but it is perfectly safe to insist that His plan is infinitely bigger and better than any we could make. We can see only the beginning of things, and that imperfectly. He can see perfectly the end from the beginning. How gladly young people should welcome a smashing up of all their puny, little plans for God's plan for their lives!

Particular reference should be made to the sacred callings, such as the ministry and other specific Christian work. These are not professions, neither are they to be chosen as professions are. They are callings, and should be engaged in by such as have been unmistakably led to them by the Holy Spirit. "Do not become a minister or missionary if you can keep away from it," may be extreme counsel, of which the other extreme advice is to "choose" one or the other of them. Be that is it may, these callings are for those on whom God lays His hand, and thrusts them out into

His vineyard. It may be all right and even necessary to submit young people to such addresses or appeals as "The Claims of the Gospel Ministry," etc., if the speaker knows how to present such a subject to young people. It may stimulate thought and help to bring about an attitude of soul which gives the Spirit an opportunity to be heard. But when all is said and done, it is He who must choose and call, and thrust out. Christ's instructions for the securing of more workers for the needy harvest field is: "Pray ye therefore the Lord of the harvest, that he send forth laborers into his harvest."—Luke 10:2. The sacred callings are His to dispense.

That person, then, who enters one of God's special and sacred callings, the ministry or other specific Christian work, should know, must know, that he is in the will of God. To this there is almost universal consent. What I now wish to declare is, that he who enters life's necessary occupations and legitimate professions may know that he is in the will and plan of God, as certainly as that one who stands behind the sacred desk or carries the Gospel to far-off heathen lands. God's voice says to some, "Go preach my Gospel," while the same voice as unmistakably says to others, as one good, Spirit-led layman once reported, "Stay at home and work." God's will was as clear to this layman, who stayed at home and engaged in an honorable occupation, as it can be to those who know that their calling is to preach. He proved it by his consistent, exemplary Christian conduct and his beautiful home-going, when his consecrated lay-life was ended.

But how shall each one find God's plan for his life? Not by remaining distant from God, closing the eyes and ears against His will. God stands ready to reveal His plan to any soul who will abandon himself in consecration to His will, and meets the conditions for holiness, so that the Holy Spirit may cleanse and completely possess and fill that heart. The vessel must be "pure," then "filled." Even, then, God does not make the whole plan clear from beginning to end. In mercy He withholds many of His plans, but reveals as much of it as is best for the consecrating soul; and then other items subsequently, according to His wisdom. In the meantime, the Spirit bears testimony to God's will and plan being wrought out in the sanctified soul, while it rests content, awaiting a further revelation of God's will.

Relative to consecration, it is to be regretted that such a superficial idea and practice is prevalent, as is evidenced in some churches and the popular young people's movements. Much of that which is called "consecration" is not consecration at all. Consecration is not the answering to a roll call, quoting a Scripture passage, giving a testimony, good as these things are. It is not a thing which must be repeated monthly or annually. It is not the giving of one's self to any cause, good or great as the cause may be. It is the complete yielding over of one's self, the absolute abandonment of the soul to God, to be His, and His alone, forever. Consecration puts the soul into the very center of the will of God, where He can begin His high and holy purposes, both to make the soul what it should be, and to use it where and as

He wills. It is man's to yield and abandon. It is God's to make and send.

Having thus found the beginning of God's plan and purpose for one's life, the next thing is to continue in His plan. Let me repeat: God in His mercy and wisdom reveals just as much of His plan to the consecrated soul as is best. It is by the devotional life or the practice of prayer, and walking in the light, that our lives are kept in God's will. Step by step, through His Word, His providences and the Spirit's leadings, we discover the unfolding plan of God for our lives. Right here, some who have once really consecrated themselves to God have failed. They neglected the means by which they might have been kept in the plan of God, and because of this have failed.

It is not likely that the devotional life will be overdone in these days of haste and anxiety. It is the almost universal experience that it is neglected. Because of this danger, special attention should be given to it. The Bible should be the constant companion, read daily and pondered over prayerfully. Childlike trust should be exercised, expecting God, through the Holy Spirit and His providences, to lead us step by step. Every available means of grace should be utilized. Stated and regular time should be set aside for secret prayer. When the writer was yet a young lad, a good man of God, taking his boyish hand in his own manly hand, and pressing it tightly, said, "Pray much." He did not then fully realize all that was contained in this brief advice, but has been learning its content ever since. He had his stated times for secret prayer, morning and evening, and now pleads guilty to a report once made of him to his Sunday School teacher, of "slipping away at noon to pray." Humbly, he should say, whatever success of a spiritual nature has been attained, what measure of clear revelation of God's plan for his life has come to him, the attempt to keep that brief but splendid bit of advice is largely responsible.

Consecration, then, is nothing short of placing the responsibility of our lives upon God, yielding over to Him our all for His glory. It is His to map out our fields, to mark out our paths and to mete out our changes. It is ours to trust implicitly and to obey completely as He reveals Himself. What a wonderful privilege it is, that we may thus shift the weighty responsibility of our lives upon one who is all-wise and all-powerful! Young people should hail such an opportunity with delight.

It is easily seen that consecration should be made early in life, so as to give God an opportunity to reveal His plan for our lives before some of our selfish little plans have been set into operation, and must be retracted from. Not only that, but if God's will and plan for life is discovered early, preparation which is so essential to greatest usefulness may be engaged in to the greatest possible advantage.

In conclusion: There are relationships, occupations, professions and callings in which holy young men and women may engage, sufficient to challenge the very best there is in the finest and most talented group of young people. A Spirit-led life, which complete consecration makes possible, puts young men and women into the plan of God and shifts the responsibility of their lives, except their obedience and trust, upon Him. It is in the Christ way where God's plan for young life and genuine success may be found.

THE CHRIST WAY IN YOUTH'S CITIZENSHIP

Chapter VIII

THE CHRIST WAY IN YOUTH'S CITIZENSHIP

It is in connection with the Christmas story, which youth knows so well, that we learn that "there was no room for him in the inn." When the Christ, to whose way youth is challenged, was born, there was no room for Him in the Roman Empire, the then-known world. No room for Him in the inn, pathetically symbolized the attitude which the world would take to Him.

Christianity was looked upon as an unlawful thing from its birth. This was not because it was beneath, but because it was above the common way of life. Following Christ made a great change, lifting the individual to a definitely higher plane.

Of the followers of Christ who were being persecuted, it is said that Saul asked of the high priest letters of authority, so that if he should find any that were of "the Way," whether men or women, he might bring them bound unto Jerusalem (Acts 9:2). It was the Christ way to which reference was made, for it was evident, even to their persecutors, that Christians had found a new way of life—something that constrained inwardly, and which was in evidence outwardly.

Many years after, when this persecutor was himself engaged in leading others into "the Way," he found those who bitterly opposed and spake evil of "the Way," and found it necessary to withdraw from them (Acts 19:9).

Jesus said to Pilate, "My kingdom is not of this world: if my kingdom were of this world, then would my servants fight."—John 18:36. Jesus also said of His followers: "They are not of this world, even as I am not of the world."—John 17:16. Paul once wrote to a group of believers in the Christ way thus: "For our citizenship (Greek, commonwealth or seat of government) is in heaven; whence also we wait for a Savior, the Lord Jesus Christ."—Phil. 3:20.

Not only was Christianity outlawed from its beginning, but it early met its bitterest competition and opposition in the form of the cult of Roman Emperor Worship. Tens of thousands of Christians, who refused to renounce their faith, and worship Rome's human god, were burned at the stake or fed to the lions in the Colosseum. The ruins of this colossal structure still stand as a solemn monument to Rome's folly and the Christian's faith. Martyr blood still courses the veins of those who follow in the Christ way.

The catacombs, still found in southern Europe and northern Africa, are silent witnesses to the secrecy with which the early Christians were compelled to promote their mutual interests. In these underground recesses, sometimes three or four stories deep, they assembled, held their services, and in these they were buried. The author recently visited, among others, the catacombs of St. Sebastian near Rome, where he saw the bones of the early followers of the Christ way lying upon the rock-hewn shelves of their catacomb tombs.

From the opposition of the world to Christianity from its beginning, and these statements made by Christ and Paul, it might appear that for those in the Christ way there is no citizenship in this world. Indeed, one of the puzzling problems for many a follower of Christ is that of his citizenship. It is of no small concern that youth should find the Christ way relative to this perplexing and age-long question of the Christian's relation to the world.

A little closer observation, however, leads to the conclusion that, though the real citizenship of the Christ way people is in heaven, they must have a temporary citizenship here. The author of the Epistle to the Hebrews, in describing the heroes of faith, wrote: "But now they desire a better country, that is, a heavenly: wherefore God is not ashamed to be called their God; for he hath prepared for them a city."— Hebrews 11:16. The comparison of a citizenship or country, which is said to be "better," suggests another, which is by comparison less or inferior.

Paul, who had been the bitter, persecuting Saul and who became, after his conversion, one of the most other-worldly of men, challenged the magistrates at Philippi who had beaten him unjustly, and had cast him into prison, by making mention of his Roman citizenship, (Acts 16:37-39). He also employed this same citizenship against the officers who were about to scourge him at Jerusalem, saying: "Is it lawful for you to scourge a man that is a Roman, and uncondemned?" Even the chief captain was frightened when he heard from Paul's lips that he was a Roman citizen. It was a prerogative of citizenship upon which Paul drew when he appealed to Caesar, when he could obtain no justice in the court at Caesarea, and was about to be sent back to Jerusalem to be tried among the prejudiced Jews. "I appeal to Caesar," were his challenging words.

Jesus, Himself, gave an example of responsibility to a temporary citizenship in this world, when He instructed Peter to cast a hook into the sea, and take the shekel which would be found in the mouth of the fish which he would catch, and pay tribute to the Roman government for Himself and Peter (Matt. 17: 27).

The first seven verses of Romans thirteen constitute a remarkable admonition on the subject of the Christian's relation to government. It begins with a command for subjection, and closes with an equally emphatic requirement for tribute, custom, fear, and honor. Rulers receive their power from God, and are God's ministers. Subjection is not to be given on account of fear only, but, by the Christian, for the sake of a good conscience. There is, then, an inescapable and moral obligation which followers in the Christ way sustain to their citizenship in this world.

A casual or superficial reading of this exhortation on the subject of citizenship discloses no qualification, whatsoever. It appears as though the Apostle Paul meant to require of those in the Christ way, an unconditional and minute obedience to rulers, irrespective of their decrees. But such cannot be the case, for there are too many illustrations to the contrary.

Three young men in Babylon refused to bow the knee to the golden idol set up by Nebuchadnezzar in the plain of Dura, though a decree was sent out by the king that they should bow and worship (Dan. 2). God was on their side, and both justified and delivered them. Daniel refused to honor the command of Darius which conflicted with his thrice daily devotion, and the God of heaven vindicated and exalted him at the expense of his jealous, plotting rivals (Dan. 6). Peter and John, forbidden by the Sanhedrin to preach any more in the name of Jesus, did not hesitate to answer: "We must obey God rather than men."—Acts 5:29.

Examining more carefully the exhortation on the duties of citizenship in question here, a qualification is found, for it is plainly stated that rulers to whom subjection is required "are not a terror to the good work, but to the evil." It is also declared that "he is a minister of God to thee for good," and that he is "an avenger of wrath to him that doeth evil." There is, then, an idealism held up for those who rule, as well as for those who are ruled. It is scarcely to be expected that God would require unqualified subjection, on the part of His people, to rulers who show no respect to Him.

The citizenship question is as old as it is new. Over it groups have quibbled, quarreled, and disagreed. It is probable that the best light thrown upon the path of those in the Christ way resulted from just such a controversy, calling forth from Jesus a great preachment.

It was upon Tuesday of Passion Week that groups were alternately attempting to snare Jesus in His words, that they might have something with which to accuse Him. Pharisees and Herodians had striven over the matter of citizenship. The contention between them was sharp, for Pharisees could never wear a yoke of foreign domination about their necks with any measure of grace, while the Herodians were sympathizers and supporters of the kingly ambitions of Herod, under the authority of Rome. Their controversy would furnish a catch question for Jesus. Both sides were anxious to incriminate Him, and there would be no way of His escape.

While we must always regret the motive which prompted the propounding of this question to Jesus, we must ever be grateful for the masterly and illuminating answer which He gave. Here is the question: "Is it lawful to give tribute to Cæsar, or not?"—Luke 20:22. If He should answer in the affirmative, He would be disloyal to His own nation subjected to Rome. If He should reply in the negative, He would be a seditionist.

Christ's answer was a dramatic one. "Show me a denarius," He demanded. "Whose image and superscription hath it?" He inquired. "Cæsar's," came the reply. It was a positive, two-sided answer, which put to silence His critics, and illumined for all time the Christ way in relation to the matter of citizenship. "Render unto Cæsar the things that are Cæsar's," is the first half of His answer. Here we can well afford to stop a moment, for there are some things which we owe to governments, typified by Cæsar. "And unto God the things that are God's," is the other half of the answer.

There are still loud and boisterous patriots who have

never discovered that there are two sides to the Christian's obligation. There are some who declare that one's debt to government and his debt to God are one and the same thing; that when one has discharged his debt to government, nothing more remains to be paid. But in the measure that Cæsar and God differed, just so far were these duties separated. In so far as political government and God are distinct today, just so there remain two sides to citizenship obligations.

This distinction is important, otherwise the multitude of martyrs, who have placed conscience and right relation to God above everything else, would have died ingloriously, and their names might well be forgotten, rather than immortalized. Certainly those who refused to respect the decrees of the Roman Government, which demanded the worship of the Emperor, retained the favor of God. Many of them were fed to the lions and burned at the stake, but are included in the World's Hall of Fame of Hebrews eleven, where they are listed as those, "Of whom the world was not worthy" (Verse 38). Were there no reality to this two-sided answer of Jesus, then obedience to the command of the Turkish rulers to slay the helpless Armenian Christians would have been morally inescapable by a subject. Then, too, all decrees of rulers would be religiously binding, regardless of their character.

The achievement of the early Christians, with all their handicap, is unparalleled in human history. Taking Jesus and His teachings seriously, outlawed as they were, with the sword sheathed from the day Christ rebuked Peter for having unsheathed it, within three centuries they had conquered the Roman Empire, and claimed its Emperor, Constantine, as a nominal convert to the Christian faith. Of course, they suffered, and many of them sealed their faith by their own blood. But what of it? Life consists not so much in how long one lives, but in how much he lives. The blood of the martyrs was, indeed, the seed of the church.

Attempting to list the items of citizenship debt, in keeping with Christ's own statements, the following results obtain:

DEBT TO GOVERNMENT

1. *Love to those who are in power.* This is evident from the command to love all, even one's enemies.
2. *Prayer for rulers.* "For kings and all that are in high place"—1 Tim. 2:2. The specific burden of this prayer immediately follows, and is worthy of note: "That we may lead a tranquil and quiet life in all godliness and gravity."
3. *Obedience to the higher powers.* (Romans 13:13.) In all matters, small and great, except in relation to such commands as conflict with the higher law of God.
4. *Tribute and custom.* Taxes imposed directly and indirectly. (Romans 13:7.)
5. *Honor of the honorable.* "Honor to whom honor." (Romans 13:7.)

DEBT TO GOD

1. *Worship.* "Thou shalt have no other gods before me"—Ex. 20:1. "Thou shalt worship the Lord thy God"—Matt. 4:10. Worship belongs to Deity alone: never to man.

2. *Service.* "Him only shalt thou serve"—Matt. 4:10. Here service is without qualification. Service to all others is necessarily on a different level.

3. *Obedience.* Man's debt of obedience to God is written all over the pages of the Bible, and is most rational. By acknowledging His creatorship, His Lordship is also conceded. Obedience to God should be yielded freely and fully, and in preference to any man. "We must (Greek, are indebted to) obey God rather than men" (Acts 5:29.)

From the very nature of man's relation to man, compared to man's relation to God, the debt owed must be different and distinct. This Jesus makes absolutely clear in His answer to the question of tribute to Cæsar. When He had answered them: "Render unto Cæsar the things that are Cæsar's, and unto God the things that are God's," it is said: "They marvelled at his answer and held their peace."—Luke 20:26.

All down the centuries Christians have sought to find the Christ way in relation to their citizenship of this world, and also to that of the other world. Success has varied, due to the nature of governments, and the perspectives followers of Christ have had upon their obligations. That these two relations could be perfectly harmonized is almost too much to expect.

Christians have always been, and continue to be, the very best citizens in any country of the world. Even when Rome was feeding them to the lions and burning them, they were the very best they had. Is there any wonder that a nation should fall, which treated her best citizens thus? Despite the fact that those of the Christ way are not always able to harmonize their lower citizenship with the higher, and might find it occasionally necessary to pay the penalty for such inability, still they remain the very choicest of citizens. Jesus even characterized them as, "the salt (preservative) of the earth". They render to Cæsar what belongs to him, and keep every law not conflicting with the law of God.

The question of active participation in government is one upon which there has not been perfect agreement by Christians. In democratic lands some Christians have been able to harmonize their relationships so as to admit of active participation in political matters. There have been others who were not able to do this, and have desisted from office holding and even from voting. Doubtless there are some men in political life who have clean hands, but it is confessedly difficult. We need good government, and how to obtain this without the positive assistance of good people is a serious problem. Strong, courageous followers in the Christ way, those who cannot be bought nor persuaded to do wrong, might make a great contribution to good government, in a country where Christian ideals are tolerated. It may be, that God will lay His hand upon some excellent young people and lead them to make a real contribution to good government. God is certainly interested in the citizenship of His people, even in this world. In no case, however, should the heavenly citizenship be jeopardized for the sake of the earthly.

Whatever may be said on these disputed points, the preachment of Jesus is as applicable today as it ever was. It is as appropriate in the occident as in the orient, and is as fundamental to the solution of the problems of citizenship in a democracy, as in a monarchy. One thing, above others, which the American youth possesses and for which he should be genuinely grateful is that of religious freedom. To be permitted to worship God, in keeping with His Word and the dictates of a good conscience, has not been conceded to Christians of all times and in all lands. May it ever be the heritage of youth in our beloved country!

The earlier that youth discovers its dual citizenship, and adjusts itself accordingly, the better. In comparison, it is the heavenly citizenship which is the real, the more important. The earthly citizenship is the temporary and less important.

The youth of America have no small problem before them, but are fortunate in that this dual citizenship can be so largely related and blended. There always has been, and there always will be, a clash between a citizenship in a world largely dominated by Satan, and one of a country where God alone rules. The challenge comes to every one in the Christ way, to meet his obligations to his temporary citizenship here, and now; but to place and hold his citizenship with God above all else, and to render to God, and to God alone, the things which belong to Him.

A closing citizenship challenge to the youth of the Christ way is found in the words of Wendell Phillips, who once, addressing a class of young men, said: "Young men, identify yourselves with some righteous, but unpopular cause." It was not that the cause was unpopular that he challenged young men to engage in it, but because it was right. Being right was likely to make it unpopular. It is the right, irrespective of popularity, into which and through which the Christ way leads.

THE CHRIST WAY IN YOUTH'S STEWARDSHIP

Chapter IX

THE CHRIST WAY IN YOUTH'S STEWARDSHIP

The Christ way and thrift are seldom associated, and to some they may appear as quite unrelated. But the Christ way and thrift are perfectly harmonious, and complement each other.

The Bible has a great deal to say about stewardship. Under the terms of money, gold, silver, talents, shekel and penny, the subject is mentioned more than a thousand times. Twice as much is said in the Bible about money as is said about prayer or faith. In relation to a subject given such prominence in the Bible, we should certainly be disappointed if there could be found no well-defined Christ way.

The basis of all Christian stewardship is God's ownership of everything—the earth and the fulness thereof (Psalm 24:1), the silver and the gold (Haggai 2:8), and all souls (Ezek. 18:4).

Since all capital belongs to God, it is His prerogative to require the payment to Himself systematically, of any proportion He chooses, in recognition of His claims of ownership. Then, too, the capital which He permits us to retain belongs to Him. Christian Stewardship is communion with God in material things.

There is no inherent piety in either poverty or plenty. We are not told that money is the root of all evil, but that the love of money is the root of all evil (1 Tim. 6:10). While an occasional person may lose his soul getting rich, hundreds lose their souls trying to get rich, but failing.

Jesus was not condemning the practice of thrift when He said: "Lay not up for yourselves treasures upon earth."—Matt. 6:19. A careful reading of these words helps to make this clear. "Lay not up", suggests the hoarding of goods in an independent manner, which is not Christian. "For yourselves", interprets the spirit in which things are frequently sought, showing that the object is purely selfish. The use of the word "treasures" leads to the inescapable conclusion, that the thing which Jesus condemned was not thrift, but a selfish hoarding of treasures for purely personal possession and use. He makes His own comment upon the statement, by saying immediately: "For where your treasure is, there will your heart be also."—Matt. 6:20. Neither was Jesus drawing a line between work and no work, between thrift and poverty, when He commanded that we take no thought for our lives (Matt. 6:25). He was drawing the line between work and worry, using the birds of the air and the lilies of the field as illustrations of being true to the law of their natures, and leaving the rest to their Creator and Preserver. Closing His comment upon the only man Jesus ever called "a fool," He said: "So is he that layeth up treasure for himself, and is not rich toward God."—Luke 12:21. This man had laid up treasures *for himself,* and herein lay his condemnation.

Despite the fact that America is a land of almost limitless opportunity for material things, the wealth of the land is in the hands of a comparative few, and the vast majority of men do not attain to a competence for old age, nor leave an estate at death which adequately cares for their families.

A United States Textbook on Thrift discloses the following facts: that of one hundred men who attain the age of twenty-five, at the age of sixty-five,

    1 is wealthy
    4 are well-to-do
    5 live on earnings
  54 are dependent
  36 are dead.

The same Textbook on Thrift gives the following figures: Of one hundred men, of all ages, who die, the estates which they leave are as follows:

    3 leave over $10,000
  15 leave $2,000 to $10,000
  82 leave no income-producing estate.

This is interpreted to mean that out of one hundred widows,

  18 are left in fairly comfortable circumstances
  47 are obliged to earn their living
  35 must depend upon charity.

There are always those who would charge their lack of material well-being to others, pointing out the greed of the rich and the oppression of the employers. Greed and oppression do exist, in varying measure, and likely will continue in a morally upside down world, and no justification is here intended for either. But knowing that such evils do exist, rendering the material well-being of the masses a more difficult proposition, it is all the more necessary that the matter of thrift should be reckoned with.

As a working definition of thrift the following is suggested: Industry, economy, and a wise expenditure and investment of income. It is in keeping with this definition that the subject of thrift is treated here.

The Christ way enjoins thrift. None would dare to dispute the fact that holy living requires the practice of industry. The Christ way and laziness are contradictory, and cannot be harmonized. The Christ way is also conducive of economy, for it frees from the slavery of some things which place a severe strain upon financial resources, such as depraved appetites, bad habits, pride, etc. The Christ way also decrees for a wise expenditure and investment of income, for it is this which transforms the individual into a prayerful, careful steward. The Christ way of heart is nothing less than union with God, through Christ, which makes communion with God in material things possible. This is Christian stewardship. The Christ way, then, instead of being foreign to the practice of thrift, actually enjoins it.

Youth is a fruitful time for the practice of thrift. It is the period of life when responsibility is less, therefore, the opportunity of reaping a larger harvest from the practice of thrift. With each succeeding year, life becomes more complex, and greater become the demands upon individual earning power. Youth is also a fruitful time for the practice of thrift, for it is the time when habits are being formed which will follow the individual through life. If thrift is practiced in early life, it is almost certain that it will be continued. If a spendthrift attitude is taken toward the financial resources of early life, it is more than

likely that the individual will find himself up against
the hard things for the rest of his days. Necessity
will drive him to his tasks, as a slave is driven, down
to old age. Even when old age comes, there may be
no way out except by continued hard labor, and
finally through charity. Old age, driven to hard toil,
presents a pathetic picture. There is certainly no
reason why young people, who belong to the Lord,
should not give attention to the matter of thrift, and
secure for themselves and their future families the
blessings which come through its adoption and
practice.

It must be remembered that "thrift" has an "if"
in it, and this "if" must be reckoned with in relation
to every item in our definition of thrift. *If* the individual will be industrious; *if* he will economize;
if he will wisely expend and invest—then and only
then he can become thrifty. The observing of any two
of these "ifs", without keeping the third, results in
failure. Remember, that an "if" meets you at every
turn of the way on the road to thrift.

Too much emphasis cannot be placed upon the wisdom of living within a margin of one's income, no
matter how small that income is. To live within the
income, only, would mean to accumulate nothing, even
for a lifetime, but just to have kept even. It would
mean no provision for the proverbial "rainy day,"
which is certain to come. Every person should so
gauge his expenditures that at least a small amount
remains over, each year. It is the only way to rise
above absolute dependence upon circumstances. Of
course, it may mean to do without some things, luxu-

ries and even needs, but it is the only way to rise. It may require rigid economy, but thrift here will pay big dividends later, when they are so much needed. Let me urge again, that it is the part of wisdom to keep the expenditures within a margin of the income, no matter how small the income is.

It is a legitimate question, how large the margin should be within which one should live, or in other words, how much should be put aside for the future, from one's income. This must be determined from the amount of income, but one-tenth should be the minimum, even from the smallest income. From a larger income, a larger margin may be saved.

The story is told that "The Richest Man in Babylon," of whom it is said that he was far-famed for his wealth; was known for his liberality; was generous in his charities and with his family; was even liberal with his own expenses in after life, came to his competency by the practice of putting aside one-tenth of his income from his young manhood, and investing the same wisely. It is marvellous what can be achieved by the practice of living within even a small margin of one's income.

Debt is often a severe handicap and, with a few possible exceptions, should be avoided. There are some things, which have a steady or constant value, which are indispensable to life, well-being and success, and which to secure require a larger sum of money than the average person could accumulate until late in life, which one is justified in obtaining on a promise of future payment. Among these might be included a home, a farm, a business, an education, professional, business or farm equipment. Even here caution is necessary, for many have found the handicap of debt, for these most constant values, too great.

Perhaps the purchase of household furniture on the deferred payment plan, in some cases, should be conceded. This concession is made reluctantly, as it would be much better if the early practice of thrift should put the home building upon another basis. It may be true that the deferred payment plan of buying household furniture is the only one which can be practiced by many young married couples, therefore, the only way for many to get started in home making. Only as a second best can the plan be conceded, and that in the interest of the home itself.

It should be strongly urged, however, that those who are compelled to finance their home making by the expensive method of the deferred payment plan, should purchase only such items as are really necessary to a comfortable home. Necessities only, not luxuries, should be purchased. Young people should free themselves from the obsession that they must begin housekeeping with all the equipment and luxuries which their parents have accumulated in a lifetime. Even young people who have the money with which to pay cash for their home furniture would do well to remember this. The young couple who together had only four hundred dollars when they were married, and who spent two hundred and seventy-five dollars for furniture, and used the balance to start a savings account, might be very profitably imitated. It is almost needless to say that this couple has never passed a year in their many years of married life, in which they have not lived within a margin of their income, and had something left over to add to their capital.

The pay-as-you-go plan has its decided advantages, and should be adopted as a fixed practice, and maintained through life. This should apply to all articles not included in the above list. Exception may be taken to insistence upon a strict pay-as-you-go plan, but those who adopt and adhere to it will find it to their decided advantage.

A popular newspaper writer recently advised that every family purchase an auto, whether they own a home of their own or not, even if they are compelled to purchase it upon the weekly installment plan. With this advice I most heartily disagree. With all sympathy for the family who is denied the pleasure and whatever profit may be derived from an auto, it should be insisted that there are several things more important than an auto. One of these is a home, a place in which to be housed and sheltered, where the family may be secure from a landlord's unkind decrees, where children may be reared for the glory of God, and for the blessing of the race.

Many a family is without home, and always will remain homeless, because of the expenditure of resources for an automobile. Some purchase them on installments, only to find that the auto is little more than a pile of junk by the time the last payment is made. If people would practice the pay-as-you-go plan in relation to autos, many would do without them entirely, and in some instances would be better off in several respects, and others would purchase autos which they can afford, instead of the expensive, luxurious cars which they cannot afford.

The pay-as-you-go plan has a decided advantage in this, that the same articles can be had at the cost of considerably less money—a cost conservatively estimated as from ten to twenty-five per cent less. A friend, engaged in the furniture business, remarked recently, that if a cash business could be done in his line, the dealer would be able to sell for twenty-five per cent less, and realize an attractive margin. This is equivalent to saying, that people who buy furniture on a deferred payment basis or on the installment plan are compelled to pay considerably more. It is no secret that credit houses sell for much higher prices, and that business concerns which sell for cash, and on credit, maintain two sets of prices.

Not long since my attention was called to a large general store in one of North America's business centers, where there is conducted what is called a "Home Lovers Club." It was reported that those who purchased from this company, through the club, were granted deferred payments, with no interest added, and no charges over the cash price which would have to be paid for the same articles in the same store. Persons who had been patronizing the credit department of this store vouched for the information.

To one interested in the study of economics and thrift, this presented an interesting problem. Immediately I sought an interview with the manager, obtaining the information that about forty thousand accounts were carried in the credit department, involving millions of dollars. In the course of conversation I insisted that if the selling price on the deferred payment plan, with no interest added, was the same as the cash price, a cash price was maintained which was higher than it should be, to make up for the expense of the credit business. To this the manager would not assent. He insisted that the high class of trade which they served, and the volume of business which the credit plan brought, justified the offering of merchandise at cash prices, on the installment plan of payment. It requires no keen-visioned economist to see that the same persons, buying the same goods with cash, should have purchased them at a saving to themselves of their share of the loss which always accompanies credit selling, also at a saving of their share of the interest on the millions of dollars involved.

It may be that an occasional situation makes the claim of this company possible, but, if so, it is the exception and not the rule. Only a very small percentage of the American people, if any at all, are fortunate enough to buy goods on the installment plan, at really cash prices.

After having studied the "Home Lovers Club" above referred to, I crossed the street to the chief competitors of the company operating the club, to find that two prices were maintained: a cash and a deferred payment price. From the daily press I then clipped an offer made by the competitors of the "Home Lovers Club," agreeing to pay ten dollars cash to any persons, and for each instance, where goods of the same quality which they offer were purchased in the city, on the deferred payment plan, for less than their cash price, plus their deferred payment charge. This exceptional situation is cited to show how unlikely it is to purchase on the installment plan at cash prices, and how universal it is that he who purchases on the deferred payment plan must suffer the handicap of extra cost.

People are only beginning to awake to the evils attendant upon credit buying. Senator James Couzens of Michigan, in an interview given out recently, said:

"Installment buying has become a national disease and a menace to sound business.

"A campaign of education of the evils attendant upon the system is necessary.

"Little emphasis has been put upon what I consider one of the chief objections to the system— that is the added cost to the article. Credit is costly. The installment buyer not only pays more but the other buyers are also affected.

"Many people are buying luxuries and doing without necessities. Investigation shows that many people are avoiding dentist and doctor bills to their own injury, in order to keep up installment payments."

The warning of Senator Couzens is being echoed by sound economists everywhere, and should be heeded.

The warning of Senator Couzens has been echoed by sound economists, and should have been heeded. Tens of thousands of families would have been in better condition for the recent depression had they not loaded themselves up with debt.

There is another serious embarrassment to the installment purchaser—that of the weekly or monthly collector. Not recounting the fact that these collectors' trips must be paid, in part, by those from whom they collect, it must be no small annoyance, to have rapping at one's door, the periodical collectors from various business houses. If there were no other incentives to the pay-as-you-go plan, it would be worth the adoption of it for the sake of being delivered from the annoyance of collectors.

Having conceded the likelihood of more or less deviation from the pay-as-you-go plan, a word concerning the matter of credit is necessary.

It is in keeping with the Christ way, that great care should be observed in the making of contracts or agreements to pay. But when such promises have been made, they should be religiously kept. One cannot afford to be a minute late in keeping a promise to pay. Promptness in paying establishes the credit of an individual. In the event payment of a promised amount is impossible at the given date, whether the obligation is a note or a verbal agreement, the creditor should be seen, and satisfactory arrangements made. Good credit is of inestimable value, and is a reflection of worthy character. Poor credit is a serious handicap to any person. Young people should be exceedingly careful to preserve a good name in relation to their stewardship, for it is more valuable than riches.

There is also a very beautiful lesson on thrift in connection with the feeding of the five thousand. After Jesus had fed the five thousand men, besides the women and children, with the five loaves and a few fishes, He gave these instructions: "Gather up the broken pieces which remain over, that nothing be lost." They then gathered up twelve baskets full. While this is not the major lesson to be learned from the feeding of the five thousand, it is one which should not be overlooked. "That nothing be lost," was our Lord's example and instructions relative to even the crumbs. Here is a splendid lesson on thrift for all time, taught by Jesus Himself.

If the Christ way enjoins thrift, as it really does, and thrift involves a wise expenditure and investment of income, then the Christ way will consider seriously how to avoid the waste of resources, and how to make them purchase the most possible for the good of mankind, and for the glory of God.

Thrift extends the ministry of Christian stewardship. He who practices thrift, and stewards for God, will have a larger amount to turn over into the Lord's treasury to help to carry on His work, and will also have an increasing amount of capital with which to do business. Here is no guarantee of wealth, but a reasonable assurance that the practice of thrift will enhance Christianity by adding to the possibility of Christian stewardship.

Thrift is enhanced by the Christ way. Just as certainly as it is true that thrift enhances the Christ way, so it is true that the Christ way enhances thrift. They complement each other. Not only does the Christ way require a systematic and scriptural recognition of God's claims of ownership upon all that we have and are, by placing a definite portion regularly into the Lord's treasury, but it also places the capital, itself, at the beck and call of God. It recognizes the fact that not only the tithe is the Lord's, but also that "the earth is the Lord's, and the fulness thereof."

There is a certain sense in which the Christ way is the safeguard to thrift. Thrift, without this ballast is cold, independent and selfish. The Christ way gives thrift a new impetus, a new motive—sanctifies it. Without holiness thrift cannot see the Lord, and seek His glory. In the Christ way, thrift glorifies God, helps to dethrone sin and exalts righteousness in the earth.